TALK BACK

TALK BACK

**A Directory
To The Addresses Of Companies
That Advertise Products
On Network Television**

THOMAS NELSON PUBLISHERS
Nashville ● Camden ● New York

Published in Nashville, Tennessee, by Thomas Nelson, Inc. and distributed in Canada by Lawson Falle, Ltd., Cambridge, Ontario.

Printed in the United States of America.

Library of Congress Cataloging in Publication Data

Main entry under title:

Talk back.

   1. Television advertising—United States—Directories.
2. Corporations—United States—Directories.
HF6146.T42T27 1983   338.7′4′02573   83-21994
ISBN 0-8407-5851-0

CONTENTS

1

2

HOW TO USE THIS DIRECTORY

This book is divided into two sections. In Section One you will find a listing in alphabetical order of individual products. Beside the name of each product you will find a number. Section Two lists in numerical order the companies that advertise on television. Each entry includes the names and addresses of the company and the products it sells. First look up the name of the product in Section One and find the number listed beside that product. Then turn to Section Two and match the number of the product with the number of the company.

If you want to comment on any given television program or any product, we suggest you write directly to the official listed with the company name in Section Two. Most advertisers appreciate hearing from viewers and customers.

Every effort was made to assure the accuracy of this list, including contacting each of the companies listed for verification of the address and product list.

SECTION ONE

Products

Find the name of the specific product being advertised in the alphabetical listing of this section and refer to the number beside the product name. Turn to Section Two, which contains a numerical listing of the companies that advertise on television, and locate the same number. The company listed beside that number is the parent company you need to contact about the product.

1

—————————————————— A

A & W root beer and fast food—1230

A T & T phone services—79

A.R.M. allergy medication—1115

A.1. Steak Sauce—1015

Aamco transmissions—6

Aapri apricot scrub—498

ABC television network—52

Absorbine Jr. liniment—1324

AC-Delco auto parts—484

Accent flavor enhancer—591

Accutron watches—721

Ace Hardware stores—11

Ace Staplers Company—51

Acme boots—879

ACT dental rinse/mouthwash —648

Active tooth polish—231

Activision video cartridges— 1354

Acu-test pregnancy test kit—142

Acutrim appetite suppressant—259

Adam computer system—272

Adams gum—1274

Adler business machines—1345

Adorn hair products—498

Advantage Series electronic telephones—478

Advil arthritis medication—63

Aerowax—63

Aetna insurance and financial services—17

Afro Sheen hair care products—649

Aftate—1071

After Eight chocolate mints—558

Agree shampoo—646

Aim toothpaste—1224

Air Force, United States—1232

Air Step shoes—195

Airwand air freshener—259

Airwick air freshener—259

Ajax detergent—274

Aladdin character kits—21

Aladdin kerosene heaters and lamps—21

Aladdin 9 to 5 lunch bag—21

Aladdin Stanley bottles—21

Aladdin thermos bottles—21

Albolene Cream—1013

Alcoa aluminum wrap—38

Alhambra bottled water—452

Alka-Seltzer—792

Alka-2—792

All Clear decongestant—170

All detergent—1224

All Ready pie crust—947

Allercreme—1274

Allerest allergy medication—926

Allied paints—1187

Allstate insurance—1089

Allsweet margarine—399

Almaden wine—842

Almond Joy candy—933

Almost Home cookies—832

Alpha Bits cereal—479

Alpine cigarettes—939

Alpo pet food—515

Alupent Mist Inhaler—1392

Always minipads and maxipads—965

Amana appliances—991

AMC automobiles—68

American Airlines—45

American Express card—56

American Gas Association—1365

American Greeting cards— 1340

American Harvest crackers— 832

American Motors automobiles—68

American Tourister luggage— 66

AMF lawn tractor—2

AMF sports equipment—2

Amore cat food—553

Amphora Blend Eleven tobacco—1248

Amway cosmetics—84

Amway household cleaning products—84

Anacin pain medication—63

Anbesol antiseptic—63

Anco wiper blades—247

Andeker beer—910

Andre champagne—468

Andre Brut champagne—468

Andre Spumanti wine—468

Andron cologne—1350

Anova Master System—337

Anso IV carpet—1391

Antonio & Cleopatra cigars— 51

Aphrodesia perfume—408

Apple computers—1368

Apple Jacks cereal—666

April Showers perfume—578

Aqua Net hair spray—408

Aqua Velva toiletries—142

Aquafilter cigarette filters— 1079

Aqua-fresh toothpaste—142

Aquamarine powder—1013

Aquarius perfume—399

Arby's restaurants—1043

Arco petroleum products— 111

Aris gloves and knitted accessories—287

Arista Records—269

Arm & Hammer baking powder—257

Arm in Arm anti-perspirant— 555

Armed Forces, United States —1232

Armed Services, United States —1232

Armor All car protection— 452

Armour meats—521

Armstrong carpets and tile— 99

Army, United States—1232

Arid deodorant—231

Arthritis Pain Formula medication—63

Artra cosmetics—1071

Aspercare aspirin—170

Aspercreme analgesic creme rub—1191

Aspergum chewing gun aspirin—1071

Assis-dent spray—188

Atari games—1273

Atlas batteries, tires, and accessories—1136

Atra razor—498

Audi automobiles—1260

Aunt Jemima pancake mix—974

Aurora bathroom tissue—53

Autolite spark plugs—1391

Aveeno skin cleanser—302

Aviance perfume—252

Avis car rentals—399

Avon cosmetics—118

Awake juice—479

Ayds reducing help—634

Aziza cosmetics—252

B.F. Goodrich tires and stores—509

B&G pickles, relishes, and sauerkraut—287

B&M Oven Baked beans—591

Babe cosmetics—408

Baby Alive toys—482

Baby Magic shampoo—781

Baby Ruth candy—832

Bache Group financial service—966

Bachman Pretzels—321

Backwoods Smoker—527

Bacon Nips snacks—930

Bactine antiseptic—792

Bagpipe tobacco—721

Bain de Soleil suntan lotion—1132

Bake-a-Bar granola bar mix—482

Baker furniture—873

Baker's chocolate—479

Bakers Joy—23

Bali women's intimate apparel—287

Balm Bar—781

Bama food products—179

Ban anti-perspirant—188

Band-Aid adhesive bandages—648

Bandits smokeless tobacco—1248

Banner toilet tissue—965

Bantron—634

Barbasol shaving cream—937

Bare Elegance—498

Bargain Hunter game—796

Bass shoes—252

Batter'n Bake cooking mix—479

Battleship game—796

Bausch & Lomb Softlens—137

Bayer aspirin—1148

BC pain powder—170

Beach 'n Beyond sportswear—527

Beacon Wax—1148

Beauty To Go hair care items 188

Beech-Nut gum—832

Beech-Nut Stages baby foods —857

Beech-Nut Tobacco—721

Beef Bite Treats dog snack— 515

Beef-a-Roni—63

Beef-o-Getti—63

Beemans gum—1274

Behoid polish—188

Bell telecommunications products and services—79

Ben-Gay rub—937

Bendix products—1391

Beneficial Finance Company —150

Beneficial Insurance—150

Beneficial National Bank—150

Bennigan's restaurants—947

Benson & Hedges cigarettes— 939

Benylin cough syrup—1274

Benzedrex—1115

Bernstein salad dressing—512

Best Foods food products— 211

Best Western motels—1288

BET-Bethlehem record label —980

Betty Crocker mixes—482

Between-the-Acts tobacco— 721

Biactrin facial cleanser—1021

Bic pens, lighters, and shavers —159

Big A auto parts—527

Big Crunch candy—857

Big Loader Construction Set —1196

Big Red gum—1302

Big Red tobacco—721

Big Time candy—287

Big Track game—796

Bill Blass shoes—1244

Binaca breath freshener—259

Birds Eye foods—479

Bisodol mints—63

Bisquick mix—482

Bit-O-Honey candy—1271

Bite-Size Tabby cat food— 1351

Biz bleach—965

Black & Decker tools—166

Black Flag insecticide—63

Black Tie cologne—649

Black Tower wine—1086

Blatz beer—552

Blitz light beer—552

Block, H & R tax consultants —169

Blue Bonnet margarine—832

Blue Lustre rug cleaner—515

Blue Plate foods—399

Blue Stratos cologne—54

BMW automobiles—121

Bo Peep ammonia—970

Body All deodorant—1148
Body Buddies—482
Body On Tap shampoo—188
Boggle game—482
Boise Cascade forest products
—175
Bold detergent—965
Bolla wine—194
Bolt paper towels—53
Bond Street tobacco—1248
Bonomo Turkish Taffee—1198
Bonz dog snacks—984
Book of the Month Club—
1193
Booth fish and seafood products—287
Borkum Riff tobacco—1248
Bounce fabric softener—965
Bountiful snack foods—1274
Bounty paper towels—965
Bourbon Blend tobacco—51
Boutique bathroom tissue—
673
Bowl Power automatic cleaner
—1148
Brach's candy—63
Brandee tobacco—321
Bravo wax—646
Brawny paper towels—53
Breacol cough syrup—1148
Breath Savers—832
Breck hair products—54
Breeze detergent—1224

Brer Rabbit molasses—1015
Breyers ice cream—337
Bridgestone tires—1393
Briggs tobacco—1248
Bright Eyes cat food—227
Brillo soap pads—970
Brim coffee—479
Brite floor wax—646
British Sterling after-shave—
1187
Bromo Quinine—188
Bromo Seltzer antacid—1274
Bronitin—63
Bronkaid asthma medication
—1148
Brooks chili hot beans—326
Brooks tangy catsup—326
Brown 'n Serve sausage—399
Bruce floor wax—521
Brunswick sporting goods—
198
Brush-Up shaving brush—498
Brut toiletries—408
Bruton tobacco—1248
Bryan meat products—287
Brylcreem hair products—142
Bubble Gum chewing gum—
832
Bubblicious gum—1274
Buc Wheats cereal—482
Buckhorn beer—910
Bud of California fresh vegetables—233

Canoe perfume—334

Canon cameras and office machines—220

Cap 10 mineral water—140

Capezio shoes—1244

Cap'n Crunch cereal—974

Capri Sun fruit drinks—287

Caravelle candy—933

Care Bears toys—482

Care-Free chewing gum—832

Carefree panty shields—648

Caress soap—1224

Carleton cigarettes—51

Carlo Rossi wine—468

Carnation food products—227

Carnu polish—646

Carpet Fresh—259

Carte Blanche credit card—116

Carter's Pills—231

Cascade detergent—965

Cashmere Bouquet soap—274

Castrol GTX motor oil—205

Catalina bathing suits and sportswear—527

Cedar King pencils—1248

Celeste Italian foods—974

Cella wine—194

Centrum vitamins—54

Century 21 real estate—1207

Cepacol mouthwash and lozenges—1021

Certain bathroom tissue—965

Certs breath mints—1274

Chambourcy yogurt—857

Chameleon sunglasses—304

Champion spark plugs—247

Chanel perfume—1352

Chantilly perfume—578

Chap Stick lip balm—1029

Chaps cologne—1273

Charles of the Ritz perfume—1132

Charleston Chew candy—832

Charley pens—1248

Charlie perfume—1013

Charm Step shoes—489

Charmin toilet tissue—965

Chaz cologne—1013

Check-Up dentifrice—800

Checkerboard foods—984

Chee-tos cheese puffs—930

Cheer detergent—965

Cheerios cereal—482

Cheez-it crackers—51

Chef Boy-ar-dee food products—63

Chef Pierre frozen pies—287

Chef's Blend cat food—227

Cheryl Tiegs sportswear—527

Chesty potato chips—321

Chevrolet automobiles—484

Chevron petroleum products—1136

Chewels gum—1274

Chex cereal—984

Chic jeans—556

Chic personal care appliances —873

Chicken In a Biskit—832

Chicken-of-the-Sea tuna—984

Chiclets gum—1274

Chief auto parts—1095

Chiffon dishwashing soap —521

Chiffon margarine—87

Child Guidance toys—210

Chimere perfume—252

Chips Ahoy cookies—832

Chips Deluxe chocolate chip cookies—665

Chiquita bananas—1230

Chit Chat crackers—832

Chloraseptic oral antiseptic and anesthetic—965

Chocks vitamins—792

Choice Morsels cat food— 984

Chooz gum—1071

Christian Brothers' wines— 1086

Chrysler automobiles—256

Chubs baby wipes—1148

Chuck Wagon pet food—984

Chuggers fruit juices—140

Chun King oriental foods— 1015

Cie perfume—54

Cinch cleaner—965

Cinemax pay cable service— 1193

Citgo gasoline stations—1095

Citicorp services—260

Citrus Hill orange juice—965

Clairol hair products—188

Clark Bar candy—140

Classic dressing—1351

Clean & Clear wax—646

Clean Rinse hair rinse—54

Clear Eyes eye medicine—7

Clearasil skin medication— 1021

Cling Free fabric softener— 142

Clorets breath fresheners— 1274

Clorox bleach—267

Clorox 2—267

Close-Up toothpaste—1224

CNA Financial insurance—721

Coast soap—965

Cobbies shoes—1244

Coca-Cola soft drink—269

Cocoa Krispies cereal—666

Cocoa Pebbles cereal—479

Cocoa Puffs cereal—482

Coffee-Mate cream substitute—227

Cold Power detergent—274

Coldene medicine—926

Coldmax cold remedy—648

Cole of California sportswear—527

Coleco games—272

Coleco Vision—272

Coleman camping equipment—273

Colgate toothpaste—274

College Inn food products—1015

Colombian coffee—279

Colombo's frozen pizza—635

Colony wines—1015

Colorex hair dye—634

Colors to Go makeup compact—399

Colorsilk hair dye—1013

Colt 45 malt liquor—1040

Columbia movies and television productions—269

Columbia Records—210

Come & Get It dog food—227

Comet cleanser—965

Comfort Stride hosiery—527

Comin' Home instant soup—217

Commodore computers—1366

Compound W wart remover—63

Comptrex cold medicine—188

Comstock Lite pie filling—326

Condition beauty pack—188

Condition shampoo—188

Condor tobacco—51

Confident denture adhesive—170

Congesperin cold medicine—188

Congoleum floor covering—284

Connect Four game—796

Connecticut General insurance—285

Connie shoes—195

Conoco gasoline—369

Contac decongestant—1115

Continental Insurance—292

Control Diet pill—1191

Converse athletic shoes—1510

Cookie Crisp cereal—984

Cool Whip whipped cream—479

Coors beer—14

Cope pain medication—1148

Copenhagen smokeless tobacco—1248

Copper-Kleen—792

Coppertone suntan products—1071

Core C 500 vitamins—792

Corelle dinnerware—304

Coricidin cough medicine—1071

Corina cigars—321

Corn Champs snacks—832

Corn Husker's body lotion—1274

Doffy Mott food products—51

Dole bananas, fresh mushrooms, and pineapple products—233

Dolly Madison cakes and pies—330

Donkey Kong cereal—984

Donkey Kong video game—272

Don Tomas tobacco—1248

Doric drink—104

Doritos corn chips—930

Double Power insecticide—1148

Double Track game—796

Doublemint chewing gum—1302

Douwe Egberts coffee, tea, and tobacco products—287

Dove detergent—1224

Dove soap—1224

Dover Farms whipped topping—479

Dow cleaner—360

Dowgard coolant—360

Downy fabric softener—965

Downyflake breakfast food—591

Dr. Granow pipes—1248

Dr Pepper soft drink—357

Dr. Scholl's foot products—1071

Dragonfire video game—1358

Drano drain opener—188

Dream Whip whipped cream substitute—479

Dreamsicle frozen confections—287

Dreft detergent—965

DRG record label—980

Dristan decongestant—63

Drive detergent—1224

Dry & Clear medicated cleanser—63

Dry Ban anti-perspirant—188

Dry Idea deodorant—498

Dry Look hair products—498

Dryad deodorants—51

Duet fudge and peanut butter patties—832

Dulcolax laxative—1392

Duncan Hines foods—965

Dungeons and Dragons video games—1372

Dunkin' Donuts—372

Duplo Products pull toys and basic building sets—701

Dupont products—369

Durabeam flashlight—337

Duracell batteries—337

Duration spray—1071

Dutch Boy paint—1103

Dutch Cleanser—970

Dutch Masters cigars—527

DX toothbrush—1224

Dynamints candy—1274
Dynamo detergent—274
E. F. Hutton—590
Eagle Brand condensed milk—179
Earth Born shampoo—498
Eastern Airlines—377
Easy To Be Me bra—527
Easy-Off oven cleaner—63
Easy-On starch—63
Eckerd Drugs—627
Ecotrin aspirin relief—1115
Edge shaving cream—646
Efferdent denture cleaner—1274
Effergrip denture adhesive—1274
El Producto cigars—527
Electrasol detergent—383
Electrolux vacuum cleaners and floor polishers—287
Elmer's Glue—179
Emeraude perfume—937
Emerson televisions—853
Emery Air Freight—391
Empire toys—746
Employers Insurance of Wausau—393
Enden shampoo—555
Endust furniture spray—188
Energizer batteries—1225
English Leather toiletries—735

Enhance perfume—646
Enjoli midnite perfume—1132
Enjoli perfume—1132
Epris perfume—881
Era detergent—965
ERA Real Estate—386
Eraser mate pens—498
Erlanger beer—651
ERO-Grato record label—980
Esoterica lotion—1013
ESPN cable TV network—495
Essence of Musk women's fragrance—735
Eureka vacuum cleaners—853
Eureka! tents—646
Evan-Picone shoes—1244
Eveready batteries—1225
Excedrin pain medication—188
Excello sportswear—527
Exelle lipstick—1029
Ex-Lax laxative—321
EXPERT BUILDER sets, accessory sets, and storage cases—701
Extend 12 cough medicine—1029
Exxon petroleum products—405
Fab detergent—274
Faberge cologne—408
Face Quencher—1029

Faiance body cream—700
Falstaff beer—413
Family Weekly magazine—210
Fancy Feast cat food—227
Fanfares shoes—195
Fantastik cleaner—815
Farm Fresh mushrooms—217
Fasteeth denture adhesive—1021
Favor polish—646
FDS feminine deodorant spray—23
Federal Express package service—422
Feen-a-mint laxative—1071
Feminique spray—188
Femiron tablets—142
Ferrari automobiles—428
FFL-Free Flight record label—980
Fiat automobiles—428
Field & Stream tobacco—1248
Fiesta deodorant soap—51
Fig Newtons—832
Figurines—947
Final Net hair spray—188
Final Touch fabric conditioner—1224
Finesse hair conditioner—555
Firehouse Jubilee tomato cocktail—887
Fireman's Fund insurance—56

Firestone tires and auto service—436
First Alert fire detector—952
First Jersey financial securities—1360
Fish Ahoy—227
Fisher-Price toys—974
Fit & Trim dog food—984
Fitch shampoo—188
Five Alive fruit drink mix—269
Flair pens—498
Flavor Plus dog food—984
FLD-Flying Dutchman record label—980
Fleischmann's margarine—832
Fletcher's Castoria laxative—1148
Flex Balsam hair conditioner—1013
Flex-Net hair spray—1013
Flintstone's vitamins—792
Florida orange juice—446
Fluffo shortening—965
Fluffy cotton candy—665
Fluorigard mouthwash—274
Flying Tiger Air Line—1356
Folger's coffee—965
Footworks shoes—195
For Bodies Only liquid soap—1013
For Brunettes Only—23

For Faces Only sun protection—1071

For Oily Hair Only hair care —498

Ford motor vehicles—451

Foremost dairy products—452

Forever Yours candy—754

Formby's wood care products —1021

Formula 409 cleaner—267

Formula 44 cough medicine—1021

Fortune magazine—1193

Foster Grant sunglasses—62

Fotomat photographic service —454

Four-Way cold tablets—188

FRAM auto parts—1391

Franco-American foods—217

Franklin Life Insurance—51

Franklin Mint collector items —1273

Free N' Soft fabric softener —383

Free Spirit bras—399

Freedent gum—1302

Freeman shoes—1244

Freezone corn remover—63

French Columbard wine—468

French's food products—459

Fresh & Lovely lipstick—1071

Fresh Horizons bread—619

Fresh Scent liquid bleach—267

Fresh Start detergent—274

Fresh Step cat litter—267

Freshen-up gum—1274

Fresh'n Dry deodorizer—188

Fresh'n Lite salad dressing mix—857

Friend's oven baked beans—591

Frigidaire appliances—1297

Friskies pet food—227

Fritos snack foods—930

Frosted Flakes cereal—666

Frosted Mini-Wheats cereal—666

Frosted Rice cereal—479

Frosting Supreme—947

Fruit Loops cereal—666

Fruit 'n Fibre cereal—479

Fruit of the Loom underwear —879

Fruit Roll-Ups—482

Fruity Pebbles cereal—479

Frye boots—23

FTD floral products by wire—448

Fudge Jumbles dessert mixes —947

Fudgsicle frozen confections —287

Fuji film—1389

Fuji magnetic tapes—1389

Fuller brushes and cleaning accessories—287

Fuller O'Brien paints—885

Future floor coating—646

Gain detergent—965

Gaines pet foods—479

Gala paper towels and napkins—53

Gallo meats—287

Gallo wines—468

Gambler fragrance—1350

Gas X—321

Gatorade soft drink—974

Gaviota ladies' swimwear—287

GDM-Gold Mind record label—980

Gee Your Hair Smells Terrific shampoo—51

General Electric (GE) products—478

General Foods International Coffees—479

General Motors parts—484

General Telephone & Electronics products and services (GTE)—487

General tires—488

Genie door opener—873

Gentle Spring douche—170

Gentle Touch skin products—51

Gentle Treatment hair relaxer—649

Georgia-Pacific wood and paper products—493

Gerber baby foods and products—494

Gerber Chunky foods—494

Geritol iron supplement—142

Getty Oil products—495

Giacobazzi wines—1304

Gillette shavers and toiletries—498

Givenchy perfume—1148

Glacier men's after-shave—1350

Glad plastic bags—1225

Glad Wrap—1225

Glade room odorizer—646

Glade Spinfresh toilet-tissue roller—646

Glamorene rug freshener—259

Glass Plus cleaner—815

Gleem toothpaste—965

Glidden paint—1051

Glo Coat floor coating—646

Gloria Vanderbilt jeans—1273

Gloria Vanderbilt perfume—1273

Glory rug cleaner—646

Hamilton Beach housewares—1081

Hamlet tobacco—51

Hamm's beer—910

Hamm's Special Light beer—910

Handi-Wrap plastic products—360

Handler shampoo—498

Handy paper towels—53

Hanes hosiery and underwear—287

Hanes Too! hosiery—287

Hangman game—796

Happy Cat "semidry" cat food—984

Happy Days smokeless tobacco—1248

Hardee's restaurants—598

Harlequin books—539

Harrah's—570

Hartz Mountain pet supplies—545

Harvest Crunch cereal—974

Harvest Wheats crackers—665

Harvey's Bristol Cream sherry—1015

Hasbro toys—546

Havoline oil—1185

Hawaiian Punch fruit drink—1015

Hawk cologne—781

Head & Chest cold remedy products—965

Head & Shoulders shampoo—965

Health-Tex clothes—252

Healthcheck instruments—1195

Heartland cereal—591

Hearty Cup O'Noodles—869

Heaven Sent all-over body spray—735

Heet liniment—63

Hefty trash bags—806

Heinekein beer—1364

Heinz food products—553

Hellmann's mayonnaise—211

Herbal Essence shampoo—188

Hero dog food—984

Hershey's chocolate products—558

Hertz car rentals—980

Hewlett-Packard electronics and computers—1333

Hi-Brand meats—287

Hi-C fruit drinks—269

Hi-Dri bathroom tissue—673

Hi-Dri household towels—673

Hi-Ho crackers-51

Hickory Farms of Ohio foods—563

Hidden Valley Ranch dressing—267

High Point coffee—965

Hills Brothers coffee—565

Hillshire Farm foods—287

Hilton hotel chain—566

Hires soft drink—965

Hitachi electronics—1339

Hold cough medicine—142

Holiday Inn motels—570

Hollywood candy—287

Home Box Office—1193

Home Insurance Company—264

Home Lite chain saws—1187

Home Pride bread—619

Home Sentry smoke alarm—478

Honda motor vehicles—64

Honey brand cereal—984

Honey-Comb cereal—479

Honeywell computers—572

Honeywell smoke alarms—572

Honor Roll pencils—1248

Hoover electric floor cleaners—574

Hoover floor washers and polishers—574

Hoover vacuum cleaners—574

Hoover washing machines—574

Hormel meats—491

Hostess snack foods—619

Hot Cycle toy—746

Hotpoint appliances—478

Houbigant perfume and cosmetics—578

Household Finance loans—582

House of Windsor tobacco—1248

Howard Johnson motels and restaurants—603

HR carpet shampooing machines—63

Hubba Bubba gum—1302

Huffy bicycles—585

Hula Chews coconut patties—63

Humpty Dumpty snack foods—51

Hungry Jack biscuits—947

Hunt tomato products—399

Hunt-Wesson foods—399

Hunter fans—1343

Hush Puppies shoes—1309

Hutton, E. F.—590

Hydra-Curve contact lens—1013

Hydrox cookies—51

IAM-I & M record label—980

I Like My Grey shampoo—188

IBM information products—611

IBM office equipment—611

Ice Trek video game—1358
Ideal toys—210
Igloo coolers—87
Imagic video games—1358
Immerse hand lotion—170
Imperial margarine—1224
Imperial shoes—1244
Impulse body spray—1224
Independent Insurance Agents —1388
Infrarub medication—63
Inglenook wines—1015
Instant Breakfast—227
Instant Fels—970
Intellevision games—766
International House of Pancakes—593
Intimate lotion—1013
Intradal personal care and household products—287
Ipso hard candies—665
Irish Red ale—14
Irish Spring soap—274
Isotoner gloves and knitted accessories—287
Isuzu automobiles—1355
Italian Swiss Colony wines—1015
ITT telephone and telegraph services—619
Ivory soap and detergent—965

J. C. Penney department stores —924
J.G. Furniture—204
J-Wax—646
Jack-in-the-Box fast foods—984
Jacob Best Premium Light beer—910
Jaguar automobiles—190
Janitor-in-a-Drum—815
Jantzen clothing—171
Jarman shoes—489
Jartran truck rentals—1353
Jax Cheese Twists snack food —321
JByrons Department Stores—627
Jean Nate toiletries—1132
Jeep automobiles—68
Jefferson Ward stores—806
Jell-O desserts—479
Jell-O fruit and cream bars —479
Jenn Air appliances—768
Jeno's frozen pizza—635
Jensen stereo equipment—399
Jergens skin care products—51
Jhirmack products—399
Jif peanut butter—965
Jiffy-Pop popcorn—63
Jim Beam whiskey—51
John Hancock Insurance—643

John Newcombe tennis wear —527
Johnson wax—646
Johnson's baby products—648
Johnson's foot products—278
Johnston's pies—1271
Jones Farm pork sausage—650
Jonker Fris fruits and vegetables—287
Jontue perfume—1013
Jordache clothing—1398
Jovan toiletries—1350
Joy detergent—965
Juice Works fruit juice drink —217
Juicyfruit chewing gum—1302
Junior Mints—832

K mart stores—655
K-Tel records—657
Kaboom cereal—482
Kahn's meats—287
Kal Kan pet food—754
Karo syrup—211
KAS potato chips—321
Kava coffee—179
Kayser intimate apparel—527
KDU-Kudu record label—980
Keebler cookies—665
Kellogg's cereals—666
Kemper insurance—732
Ken-L-Ration pet food—974
Kendall Oil products—1308

Kenmore appliances—1089
Kenner toys—482
Kent cigarettes—721
Kentucky Club tobacco—321
Kentucky Fried Chicken— 1015
Kero-Sun heaters—1357
Key tobacco—1248
Kibbies & Bits pet food—974
Killian's Irish Red ale—14
Kindness hair dryer—188
Kindness Soft Perm—188
King Vitamin cereal—974
Kingsford charcoal—267
Kinney Shoes—1313
Kit Kat candy—558
Kitchen Bouquet—267
KitchenAid appliances—337
Kitten Food—227
Kitty Clover potato chips— 321
Kix cereal—482
Kjirst malt beverage—1224
Klear floor coating—646
Kleen Guard—23
Kleenex bathroom tissue— 673
Kleenex facial tissue—673
Kleenex household towels— 673
Kleenex Huggies disposable diapers—673

Liberty Mutual Insurance—713

Life cereal—974

Life game—796

Life Savers candy—832

Life Stride shoes—195

Lifebuoy soap—1224

Lifeline Professional toothbrushes—1224

Lifestage vitamins—1021

Light Chablis wine—842

Like caffeine-free cola—939

Lincoln Continental automobiles—451

Lip Quencher—1029

Lipton Egg Noodle—1351

Lipton tea and soups—1351

Liqua 4 liquid soap—521

Liquid Cream Soap—1350

Liquid Plumr drain opener—267

Listerine mouthwash—1274

Listermint mouthwash—1274

Lite beer—939

Litter Green cat litter—267

Little Friskies cat food—227

Litton ovens—717

Liz Claiborne ladies' apparel—527

Liz Claiborne shoes—1244

Lo-Sal antacid tablets—1148

Loews theatres and hotels—721

Log Cabin syrup—479

London Dock tobacco—321

Long & Silky hair conditioner—188

Long John Silver's Seafood Shoppes—722

Longfresh Thundermint chewing gum—665

L'Oreal hair care products—306

Louis Rich meats—479

Love My Carpet—1148

Loving Care hair care—188

Lowenbrau beer—939

Lubriderm lotion—1274

Lucite paint—369

Lucky Charms cereal—482

Lucky Strike cigarettes—51

Lucky 100's cigarettes—51

Luv's diapers—965

Lux dishwashing detergents—1224

Lux soap—1224

Lyon's restaurants—287

Lysol disinfectant—1148

M & M's candy—754

M-Network video cartridge—766

Macleans toothpaste—142

Madison Square Garden sports and entertainment organization—527

Magic Blend dressing—326

Magic Chef appliances—742

Magnavox television and audio-video centers—873

Main Stay dog food—984

Mallory batteries—745

Manhandler soups—217

Manischewitz wines and foods —749

Mapleton tobacco—1248

Marabou milk chocolate roll— 558

Marathon mascara—884

Mariner outboard motors— 198

Marines, United States—1232

Mark IV tobacco—1248

Marlboro cigarettes—939

Marquiese shoes—195

Marriott hotels—1382

Mars candy—754

Mary Kay cosmetics—759

Maryland Club coffee—269

Mason Dots & Crows—1198

Masonite wood products—762

Massengill douches—142

Masson wines—1086

MasterCard credit cards—604

Master Lock—51

Matchlight charcoal—267

Mattel Electronics—766

Mattel Toys—766

Max cigarettes—721

Max Factor cosmetics—881

Max hair dryer—498

Max-pax coffee—479

Maxi by Max Factor—881

Maxim coffee—479

MAXITHINS sanitary pads —1176

Maxwell House coffee—479

Maybelline cosmetics—1071

Maytag appliances—768

Mazda automobiles—769

Mazola vegetable oil and margarine—211

McCormick spices, condiments, and flavorings—770

McCulloch power saws—166

McDonald's fast food—771

Mead school supplies—777

Mealtime dog food—754

Mego toys—778

Megomania video game— 1354

Meister Brau beer—939

Mellow Roast coffee—479

Memorex computers—207

Memorex recording tape— 1177

Mennen after-shave—781

Mentholatum—782

Meow Mix cat food—984

Mequiar's Fast Finish car polish—1397

Mercedes-Benz automobiles and buses—783

Mercury automobiles—451

Mercury outboard motors—198

Merit cigarettes—939

Merit towels—965

Merle Norman cosmetics—785

Merlin game—482

Merrill Lynch investments—786

Metrecal diet food—188

MG automobiles—190

MGM/UA movie and television productions—1380

Micatin foot spray—648

Michelin tires—790

Michelob beer—88

Michelob Light beer—88

Micro-Vision game—796

Microsurgeon video game—1358

Midas auto parts—591

Midol pain medication—1148

Mighty Dog pet food—227

Milford Plaza Hotel—1288

Milk-Bone pet food—832

Milk-Mate chocolate syrup—1015

Milk Shake candy—287

Milky Way candy—754

Miller beer—939

Millionaire cologne—781

Milton Bradley games—796

Mini-Wheats cereal—666

Mink Difference shampoo—498

Mink hair spray—498

Minolta cameras and office machines—799

Minute Maid orange juice—269

Minute Rice—479

Minute Wax—1217

Miracle Gro fertilizer—1151

Miracle margarine—337

Miracle Whip spread—337

Mirro aluminum products—803

Miss Clairol hair products—188

Miss Den cosmetics and personal care products—287

Missing Links game—210

Missoni fragrance—339

Mister Big paper towels—493

Mister Brau beer—939

Mistol nasal drops—1071

Mitchum anti-perspirant—1013

MLN-Millennium record label—980

Mobil oil products—806

Moccomat food service coffee and beverage systems—287

Moisture Tanning Face Cream—1132

Moisture Wear make-up—884

Mojud hosiery—527

Momentum pain medication —63

Monroe shock absorbers— 1184

Montclair cigarettes—51

Mongomery Ward stores—806

Moon Drops lipstick—1013

Mop & Glo floor cleaner— 1148

Morton salt—815

Morton's frozen foods—1015

Most cereal—666

Motorcraft automotive parts— 451

Motorola television—765

Motts fruit products—51

Mounds candy—933

Mountain Dew soft drink— 930

Mr. & Mrs. T. Cocktail Mix —51

Mr. Clean cleaner—965

Mr. Coffee coffeemaker—874

Mr. Goodbar candy—558

Mr. Goodwrench service—484

Mr. Mouth game—1196

Mr. Muscle oven cleaner— 188

Mr. Whisk wet/dry shaver— 765

Mrs. Butterworth's syrup— 1224

Mrs. Dash salt-free seasoning —23

Mrs. Goodcookie cookies— 553

Mrs. Paul's frozen foods— 217

Mrs. Smith's pies—666

Multifilter cigarettes—939

Mum deodorant—188

Muralo paint and stain—882

Muriel cigars—527

Murine eye drops—7

Musk after-shave—832

Mustang pens—1248

Mutual Benefit Life insurance —369

Mutual of Omaha insurance —831

My-T-Fine pudding and pie filling—1015

Myadec vitamins—1274

Nabisco foods—832

Nair hair remover—231

Nallys chili products—326

NAPA auto parts—833

National car and truck rentals —582

National Enquirer tabloid newspaper—843

Nationwide Insurance—855

Natural Gas fuel—929

Natural Light beer—88

Natural Pizza—635

Natural Wonder cosmetics—1013

Naturalizer shoes—195

Naturally Blonde shampoo—188

Nature Scents soap—51

Nature Valley Fruit Squeez juices—482

Nature Valley granola bars—482

Navy, United States—1232

Nawico wines—1248

NBC television network—980

NCL Cruise Lines—1385

Necta Sweet saccharin—965

Neet hair remover—63

Neo-Synephrine decongestant—1148

Nerf toys—482

Nescafe coffee—857

Nestea tea—857

Nestle's food products—857

New Breed dog food—227

New Eyes eye makeup remover—287

New Freedom feminine pads—673

Newport cigarettes—721

New Trail granola bars—558

New York Life Insurance Company—862

Niagara starch—211

Nice cough lozenges—142

Nice 'n Easy shampoo—188

Night Musk fragrance—252

Nikon cameras—1374

9-Lives cat food—553

Nissan motor vehicles—868

Nivea skin cream and lotion—144

No Escape video game—1358

No More Tangles—648

No Salt flavoring—1013

No-Doz medication—188

No-Nonsense hosiery—527

No-Pest Strip and liquid insecticide—815

Nordic Ware—877

Norelco shavers and appliances—873

Norforms feminine hygiene products—965

Northern bathroom tissue and paper napkins—53

Northwestern Mutual life and disability income insurance—880

Norwich aspirin—965

Norwich glycerin suppositories—965

Novahistine—360

Noxzema Continuous Protection Cream—884

Noxzema skin cream—884

NP-27 athlete's foot care—965

Nuance perfume—937
Numbers Up game—796
Nutone housing products—1081
Nutri Sweet—1088
Nutri-tonic shampoo—344
Nutri-Grain cereal—666
Nuts About Fruit bars—482
NyQuil decongestant—1021
Nytol sleeping pills—170

O. B. tampons—648
Oasis deodorant—965
Oatmeal Fudge cookies—832
Ocean Spray cranberry products—887
Odor Eaters—278
Odyssey video games—873
Off insect repellent—646
Ogilvie Home Permanent—1148
O'Gradys potato chips—930
Oil of Olay lotion—1021
Old El Paso Mexican foods—591
Old English oil—63
Old Gold cigarettes—721
Old Milwaukee beer—651
Old Milwaukee Light beer—651
Old Spice toiletries—54
Old Style beer—552
Olde English 800 beer—910
Oldsmobile automobiles—484

Olin H-T-H pool chemicals—892
Olympia beer—910
Olympia Gold beer—910
Olympic paints—882
Olympus cameras—898
Omega band instruments—873
Omega fishing reels—198
Omega tobacco—721
On Guard bowl cleaner—259
100% Bran cereal—832
One Step at a Time-Water Pik—1182
One Touch—1347
One-A-Day vitamins—792
Oneida silversmiths—896
Onesies underwear—494
Open Air room odorizer—1100
Operation game—796
Ora Brite—1013
Ora Fix denture adhesive—1013
Oral-B Zendium toothpaste—302
Orange juice from Florida—446
Orange Plus orange juice—479
Orbit gum—1302
Ore Ida potato products—553
Oreo cookies—832

Organics shampoo and conditioner—408

Orkin Pest Control—1033

Ortega chiles—1015

Orville Redenbacher's popping corn—399

Oscar de le Renta menswear—527

Oscar Mayer meats—479

Ovaltine malt drink—1062

Oven Fry—479

Oven Guard—188

Owens-Corning insulation—905

Oxford chemicals—287

Oxydol detergent—965

Paas Easter egg colors—1071

PAB-Pablo record label—980

Pabst Blue Ribbon beer—910

Pabst Extra Light beer—910

Pabst Special Dark beer—910

Pac Man Table Top game—272

Pace pool products—892

Paine-Webber brokers—911

Paladin Blackcherry tobacco—51

Pall Mall cigarettes—51

Palmolive soap and detergent—274

Palter shoes—195

Pam cooking spray lubricant—63

Pampers diapers—965

Pamprin medication tablets—250

Pan American airways—914

Panadol pain reliever—1148

Panasonic televisions—765

PAN-Panorama record label—980

Paper Mate pens—498

Pappagallo shoes—1244

Paramount Pictures movies—527

Parkay margarine—337

Parker Brothers games—482

Parliament cigarettes—939

Pascalle fragrance—527

Patio Mexican foods—1015

Paul Masson wines—1086

Paul Revere Life Insurance—116

Payday candy—287

Peak antifreeze—876

Pearl Drops tooth polish—231

Pearle Vision Eye Centers—1088

Pebbles cereal—479

Peerless faucets—760

Pencil Pets—1196

Penetreat hair care—1148

Penney's department stores—924

Pennzoil motor oil—927

Pentax binoculars—1335
Pentax cameras—1335
Pentax video—1335
People magazine—1193
Pepperidge Farm foods—217
Pepsi-Cola soft drink—930
Pepsodent toothbrushes—1224
Pepsodent toothpaste—1224
Pepsodent tooth powder—1224
Pepto-Bismol—965
Perk floor wax—1148
Perkins restaurants—570
Permalens—302
Permasoft shampoo and conditioner—857
Personal Pan Pizza—930
Personal Touch lady's razor—1274
Pert shampoo—965
Pertussin cold medicine—252
Pet Evaporated milk—591
Peter Pan peanut butter—399
Peter Paul candy—933
Peter Piper pizza restaurants—521
Phase III soap—1224
Philco televisions—873
Philip Morris cigarettes—939
Phillips Milk of Magnesia—1148
Phillips petroleum products—940

pHisoDerm medicated cleanser—1148
Piels beer—651
Piels Light & Draft Style beer—651
Pierre Cardin toiletries—54
Pillsbury mixes—947
Pine Power cleaner—815
Pine-Sol cleaner—54
Pioneer stereo equipment—1529
Pivot pool game—796
Pizza Hut restaurants—930
Pizza Quick—252
Pizzazz makeup—118
Planters peanuts—832
Players cigarettes—939
Playmobil toys—1375
Playtex garments—399
Playtop undergarments—399
Pledge wax—646
Plunge drain opener—188
Plush carpet cleaner—259
Plymouth automobiles—256
PNT-Planet record label—980
Polar Caps ice cream and cookie sandwiches—337
Polaroid cameras—955
Poli-grip denture adhesive—170
Polident denture cleaner—170
Pollenex Dial Massage showerheads—107

Polo Brindisi wine—468

Pommerelle wines—1248

Pond's skin cream—252

Pontiac automobiles—484

Pop Polish nail enamel—252

Pop-Tarts—666

Popeye children's vitamins—142

Poppin Fresh dough—947

Popsicle frozen confections—287

Porcelana cream—634

Porsche automobiles—1260

PortaTap boxed wine—1015

Post cereals—479

Postum cereal—479

Posturepedic mattress—1087

Potato 'n Sesame snack thins—832

Praise dog food—984

Praise soap—1224

Preference hair dye—306

Prego spaghetti sauce—217

Prell shampoo—965

Premesyn tablets—252

Premium Saltines crackers—832

Preparation H hemorrhoid medication—63

Prescribe Nail Care—1132

Presto appliances—849

Prestone antifreeze—1225

Pretty As A Picture air freshener—1148

Pride wax—646

Primatene asthma medication—63

Prime dog food—479

Primo beer—651

Prince Matchabelli toiletries—252

Prince tennis racquets—252

Pringle's potato chips—965

Pritikin low-salt foods—1191

Product 19 cereal—666

Prolamine—1191

Promise spreads—1224

Promise toothpaste—170

Protectall clear vinyl sheet protector—1396

Protein 21 shampoo—781

Protein 29 hair products—781

Prudential Insurance—966

Publishers Clearing House—968

Pudding Bars—179

Puffed Wheat cereal—974

Puffs tissue—965

Puppy Chow dog food—984

Puppy Formula dog food—227

Purex bleach—970

Purex detergent—970

Purina pet food—984

Puritan cooking oil—965
Purolator courier service—972
Purolator filters—972
Pursettes tablets—634
Pursettes tampons—634
Puss 'n Boots cat food—974
PYA/Monarch food service distribution—287

QPB books—1193
Q-tips—252
QT suntan lotion—1071
Quaker cereals—974
Quaker Chewy granola bars —974
Quaker State motor oil—975
Quasar television sets—765
Quiet Touch hair care—188
Quik drink mix—857
Quik Mart convenience stores —1095

Radio Shack stores, electronics and computers—1177
Ragú Italian foods—252
Raid insecticide—646
Rain Barrel fabric softener— 646
Raintree skin cream—884
Raleigh bicycles—982
Ramada Inns motels—985
Ramblin' Root Beer—269
Rapid-Shave shaving cream —274

Rave hair care—252
Ray-O-Vac batteries and lighting devices—599
RC Cola soft drink—1043
RCA television sets—980
RDS-Roadshow record label —980
Reach toothbrush—648
ReaLemon lemon juice—179
Red Devil paint—608
Red Lobster restaurants—482
Red Man chewing tobacco— 515
Red Seal tobacco—1248
Reese's candy—558
Regal shoes—195
Rejoice liquid soap—965
Remington appliances—1129
Remington shaver—1129
Renault automobiles—68
Renuzit freshener—188
Replay gum—832
Rescue soap pads—798
Resolution II diet tablets— 700
Resolve cold gel—360
Revelation Tobacco—1248
Revlon cosmetics—1013
Reynolds aluminum products —1016
Rhine light wine—1086
Rice Chex cereal—984

Rice Krispies cereal—666

Ricoh Copier Machine 4060 —1384

Riddle of the Sphinx video game—1358

Right Cut tobacco—1248

Right Guard anti-perspirant— 498

Rinse Away shampoo—231

Rinso detergent—1224

Rise shaving cream—231

Ritz crackers—832

Riunite wine—127

Rival appliances—1025

Rive Gauche perfume—1132

Robert Burns cigars—321

Robitussin cough medicine— 1029

ROC-Rocket record label— 980

Rockwell tools—1030

Roi Tan cigars—51

Rolaids antacid—1274

Rolo candy—558

Roman Meal bread—1271

Rooster tobacco—1248

Rose Milk skin care lotion— 142

Round-the-Clock hosiery— 399

Roverolli dog snack—984

Royal business machines— 1345

Royal Comfort pipe tobacco —1015

Royal Danish tobacco—321

Royal Oak charcoal—493

Royal pudding—832

Royals mint chocolates—754

Rubbermaid products—1045

Rubik's Cube—210

Rudy's Farm meats—287

Ruffles potato chips—930

RusEttes frozen potato products—287

Rust-Oleum rust preventive coating—1049

Ryder Truck Rental—1050

S.B. Thomas' English Muffins—211

S.O.S. soap pads—792

Safeco Insurance—1055

Safeguard soap—965

Sail Aromatic tobacco—51

Sal Hepatica—188

Sally Hansen's Hard-as-Nails —344

Saluto Deep Dish Pizza—482

Sambo's Restaurants—1059

Samsonite luggage—140

Sandcastle sportswear—527

Sani-Flush toilet cleaner—63

Sanka coffee—479

Sara Lee frozen baked goods —287

Sarah Coventry jewelry—1155

Sentry insurance—1092

Serengeti sunglasses—304

Sergeant's pet supplies—1029

Serta mattresses—1093

Serutan tonic—832

Sesame crackers—832

7-Eleven convenience stores —1095

Seven Seas salad dressings— 87

Seven-Up soft drink—939

Shake 'n Bake meat coating mix—479

Shakespeare cigars—321

Shape 'n Shadow eye kit— 937

Sharp computers, copiers, business machines, microwave ovens, televisions, video cassette recorders, audio equipment—1098

Shasta soft drinks—287

Shedd's Spreads—140

Sheer Elegance hosiery—287

Sheer Energy hosiery—287

Shell pesticides—1100

Shell oil products—1100

Sheraton hotels—619

Sherwin-Williams paint and carpet—1103

Shield soap—1224

Ship 'n' Shore clothing—482

Shooting Gallery video games —1358

Short & Sassy shampoo—188

Shout stain remover—646

Shower Dew liquid soap— 170

Shower to Shower body powder—648

ShowerMate soap—800

Showtoons boys' underwear— 287

Shredded Wheat cereal—832

Signal mouthwash—1224

Signature beer—651

Silence Is Golden cough syrup —188

Silhouette Books—527

Silkience—498

Silva Thins cigarettes—51

Similac baby food—7

Simmer Soup—857

Simmons mattresses—527

Simon & Schuster publishers —527

Simon game—796

Simonize car care products —1225

Sinarest decongestant—926

Sine-Aid sinus medication— 648

Sine-Off decongestant—1115

Sinex—1021

Suave shampoo—555
Subaru automobiles—1159
Sucaryl sweetener—7
Sucrets lozenges—142
Sudden Tan lotion—1071
Sugar Crisp cereal—479
Sugar Pops cereal—666
Sugar Smacks cereal—666
Sugar Twin sweetener—23
Suisse Mocha coffee—479
Summer's Eve douche—443
Summit cookie bars—754
Summit towels—965
Sun Sensor sunglasses—304
Sun-drop soft drink—965
Sun-Maid raisins—1164
Sunbeam kerosene heaters—28
Sunkist oranges—1166
Sunlight dishwashing liquid—1224
Sunlite sunflower oil—881
Sunny Delight drink—104
Sunoco gasoline—1161
Sunrise instant coffee—857
Sunshine biscuits—51
Super Dry disposable diapers—673
Super Net hair spray—689
Super Pop popcorn—326
Super Romance books—539
Super Simon game—796
Super Suds soap—274

Super Sugar Crisp cereal—479
Superior food service coffee and tea—287
Supermax hair dryer—498
Supp-hose stockings—527
Sure & Natural sanitary napkins—648
Sure anti-perspirant—965
Surround cough syrup—1021
Suzuki motor vehicles—1247
Swan dishwashing detergent—1224
Swanson prepared foods—217
Sweet Heart bar soap—970
Swift's meats and meat products—399
Swingline Stapler—51
Swiss Miss pudding and frozen pudding bars—140
Swords and Serpents video games—1358
Sylvania televisions and audio-video centers—873
T-Zone cold remedy—231
Ta-Tos potato chips—930
Tab soft drink—269
Tabu perfume—334
Taco Bell fast food—930
Take-Off makeup remover towels—648
Talker camera—799
Tame hair products—498

Tops Sweet tobacco—321
Tor-Ticos tortilla chips—321
Toss N Soft fabric softener—970
Tostitos tortilla chips—930
Total cereal—482
Total Dinner cat food—1351
Touch of Class cologne—408
Touch of Scent air freshener—1079
Town House crackers—665
Toyota motor vehicles—1205
Trac Drive garage door openers—873
TracII shaving products—498
Trail mix bars—227
Transamerica Insurance—1208
Trans World Airlines—1207
Treasure Cove salad dressing—399
Tree Top apple juice—1341
Trend detergent—970
Triaminic cough formula—1062
Trick Shot video games—1358
Tricot Mesh Band-Aids—648
Trident chewing gum—1274
Trim diet soup mixes—1224
Triscuit snack crackers—832
Triumph automobiles—190
Triumph cigarettes—721
Trix cereal—482

Tronolane medication—7
TropArtic batteries and oil—940
Tropical Blend suntan lotion—1071
Tropicana orange juice—140
Tru-Value hardware stores—307
Truckin' video games—1358
True Brunette hair dye—188
True cigarettes—721
True Reflections pantyhose—287
TRW businesses—1173
TSR hobbies and video games—1372
Tuffy cleaning pads—792
Tums medication—1013
Tupperware plastic containers—337
Turbo men's fragrance—408
Turco kerosene heaters—1362
Turtle Wax—1217
Tussy deodorant—1148
20th Century Fox films—1377
24 Hour deodorant—689
Twice as Fresh deodorizer—267
Twice as Nice shampoo—1224
Twinkle metal polish—188
Twix candy—754
Twizzlers candy—558

51

2 in 1 Plus Reflecting Collars—545

Tyco toys—287

Tylenol pain medicine—648

Tyson Breast of Chicken—1219

TZ-3 athlete's foot ointment—937

U-Haul truck and trailer rentals—44

Ultima II cosmetics—1013

Ultra Ban anti-perspirant—188

Ultra Brite toothpaste—274

Ultra Lean diet aid—1191

Ultra Sense hosiery—527

Ultra Sheen hair products—649

Ultrex blades—1274

Uncle Ben's rice—754

Underalls ladies' hosiery—287

Underwood meat spreads—591

Unguentine first aid and sunburn products—965

Unicap vitamins—1251

Uniflo motor oil—405

Union Carbide—1225

Union Leader tobacco—1248

Union Oil Company—1227

Union refined sugar—287

Uniroyal tires—1228

Unisom—937

United Air Express—1220

United Airlines—1220

United Artist film and television productions—1380

United States Air Force—1232

United States Armed Forces—1232

United States Armed Services—1232

United States Army—1232

United States Marines—1232

United States Navy—1232

Universal Motion Pictures—1378

Uno cards—1383

V-8 vegetable juice—217

Vagisil lotion—278

Valu-Rite drug stores—452

Valvoline motor oil—103

Van Dyck tobacco—321

Vanish toilet cleaner—188

Vanquish pain medication—1148

Vaporub cough drops—1021

Vaseline products—252

Vectrex video games—766

Vel detergent—274

Velamints breath mints—983

Velveeta cheese—337

Vermond Maid maple syrup—1015

Vibrant bleach—965

Vic 20 Commodore computers —1366

Vicks medications—1021

VIC-Victor record label—980

Vidal Sassoon hair products —1021

Viking tobacco—321

Virginia Slims cigarettes—939

VISA credit card—129

Visine eye drops—937

Vitabank vitamins—142

Vitabath bath products—1350

Vitalis toiletries—188

Viva corn chips—321

Viva paper towels—1078

Vivante wine—269

Vivarin stimulant tablets—142

Vive la Dijon mustard—459

Vlasic pickles—217

VO 5 hair products—23

Volkswagen automobiles— 1260

Volvo automobiles—1262

VTR-Victrola record label— 980

Wagner Power Sprayer—1264

Walgreen Drug Stores—1266

Wall Street men's fragrance— 735

Wall-Mount hair dryers—873

Wang Labs computers, word processing systems, and of-fice automation equipment —1270

Warner Communications prod-ucts—1273

Wash 'n Dri disposable tow-els—274

Water Pik shower massage— 1182

Wausau insurance—393

Wave dry bleach—267

WB Cut tobacco—1248

WDN-Wooden Nickel record label—980

WDS-Windsong record label —980

Wear-Ever appliances—38

Weber grills—1347

Weight Watchers foods and classes—553

Welch's grape products—1280

Welch's soft drink—357

Wella hair products—1282

Wendy's hamburgers—1286

Wesson vegetable oil—399

Western Airlines—1287

Western Auto stores—150

Western Electric telephone equipment—79

Westinghouse products—1291

Wet Ones moist towelettes— 1148

Whatchamacallit candy—558

Wheat Chex cereal—984

Wheat Thins crackers—832

Wheaties cereal—482

Wheatsworth crackers—832

Whirlpool appliances—1294

White Cloud tissue—965

Whitehall tobacco—321

White Owl cigars—321

White Rain shampoo—498

Whitman's chocolates—591

Whitney's yogurt—666

Widget all-purpose tool—498

Wildroot hair dressing—274

William Penn cigars—321

Williams Lectric Shave lotion —142

Wilson sporting goods—930

Winchell's Donut Houses— 347

Wind Song perfume—252

Windex glass cleaner—188

Wish-Bone salad dressing— 1351

Wisk detergent—1224

Wizard room deodorizer—63

Wolf Brothers tobacco—1248

Wonder Bread—619

WonderBra intimate apparel —287

Wondra hand lotion—965

Wood Plus furniture polish— 815

Woodbury soap—51

Woolite laundry products— 63

Word Christian Book Publishers—52

Work Horse chewing tobacco —1015

Worksoap—800

Wrangler boots—171

Wrangler clothes—171

Wrigley's chewing gum—1302

Wyler's beverages and soups —179

Xerox office machines and supplies—1319

Yahtzee game—796

Yale security products—1081

Yamaha motorcycles—1321

Yardley soaps—1350

Yes liquid laundry detergent —815

Yoplait yogurt—482

York Peppermint Pattie candy —933

You Form It women's wear— 489

Youth Garde moisturizing cream—63

Yuban coffee—479

Yves St. Laurent cosmetics —1132

Zales stores—1325

Zaxxon video games—272

Zebco fishing reels—198
Zenith microcomputers, television sets, and electronics—1327
Zerex antifreeze—369
Zero candy—287

Zest detergent bar—965
Zesta crackers—665
Zestabs—170
Ziploc bags—360
Zippo lighters—1330

SECTION TWO

Advertisers

This section contains a listing of network advertisers in numerical order. First look in Section One for the individual product being advertised. Then match the number beside that product with the same number in this section. The company listed is the parent company of the product.

2—AMF, Incorporated, Pres. Eldon E. Fox, 777 Westchester Ave., White Plains, NY 10604, Phone 914-694-9000. **PRODUCTS:** AMF lawn tractor. AMF sports equipment.

6—AAMCO Automatic Transmissions, Inc., Pres. Robert Morgan, 408 E. 4th St., Bridgeport, PA 19405, Phone 215-277-4000. **PRODUCTS:** Aamco transmissions.

7—Abbott Laboratories, Chrm. Robert A. Schoellhorn, Abbott Park, North Chicago, IL 60064, Phone 312-937-6100. **PRODUCTS:** Clear Eyes eye medicine. Murine eye drops. Selsun Blue shampoo. Similac baby food. Sucaryl sweetener. Tronolane medication.

11—Ace Hardware Corporation, Chrm. Theodore Costoff, 2200 Kensington Ct., Oak Brook, IL 60521, Phone 312-887-6600. **PRODUCTS:** Ace Hardware stores.

14—Adolph Coors Company, Chrm. William K. Coors, Golden, CO 80401, Phone 303-279-6565. **PRODUCTS:** Coors beer. Golden Lager 1873. Killian's Irish Red ale.

17—Aetna Life & Casualty, Chrm. John H. Filer, 151 Farmington Ave., Hartford, CT 06156, Phone 203-273-0123. **PRODUCTS:** Aetna insurance and financial services.

21—Aladdin Industries, Inc., Chrm. V.S. Johnson, Jr., 703 Murfreesboro Rd., Nashville, TN 37210, Phone 615-748-3000. **PRODUCTS:** Aladdin character kits. Aladdin kerosene heaters and lamps. Aladdin 9 to 5 lunch bag. Aladdin stanley bottles. Aladdin thermos bottles.

23—Alberto Culver, Pres. Leonard H. Lavin, 2525 Armitage Ave., Melrose Park, IL 60160, Phone 312-450-3000. **PRODUCTS:** Bakers Joy. FDS feminine deodorant spray. For Brunettes Only. Frye boots. Kleen Guard. Mrs. Dash salt-free seasoning. Sparklers air freshener. Static Guard. Sugar Twin sweetener. VO 5 hair products.

28—Allagheny International Corporation, Chrm. Robert J. Buckley, P.O. Box 456, Pittsburgh, PA 15230, Phone 412-562-4000. **PRODUCTS:** Sunbeam kerosene heaters.

38—Aluminum Company of America, Chrm. C. W. Perry, 1501 Alcoa Building, Pittsburgh, PA 15219, Phone 412-553-4545. **PRODUCTS:** Alcoa aluminum wrap. Wear-Ever appliances.

44—Amerco, Chrm. L.S. Shoen, 2727 N. Central Ave., Phoenix, AZ 80004, Phone 602-263-6011. **PRODUCTS:** U-Haul truck and trailer rentals.

45—American Airlines, Inc., Chrm. Albert V. Casey, P.O. Box 61616, Dallas, TX 75261, Phone 817-355-1234. **PRODUCTS:** American Airlines.

51—American Brands, Inc., Chrm. Edward W. Whittemore, 245 Park Ave., New York, NY 10017, Phone 212-557-7000. **PRODUCTS:** Ace Staplers Company. Cheez-it crackers. Dark Eyes vodka. Doffy Mott food products. Dryad deodorants. Fiesta deodorant soap. Franklin Life Insurance. Gee Your Hair Smells Terrific shampoo. Gentle Touch skin products. Hi-Ho crackers. Humpty Dumpty snack foods. Hydrox cookies. Jergens skin care products. Jim Beam whiskey. Krispy crackers. Master Lock. Motts fruit products. Mr. & Mrs. T. Cocktail Mix. Nature Scents soap. Spey Royal Scotch. Squeak! shampoo. Sunshine biscuits. Swingline Stapler. Woodbury soap. **CIGARETTES:** Cadets. Carlton. Lucky 100's. Lucky Strike. Montclair. Pall Mall. Silva Thins. Tareyton. Thins 100's. **TOBACCO PRODUCTS:** Antonio & Cleopatra cigars. Bourbon Blend. Condor. Half & Half. Hamlet. La Corona cigars. Paladin Blackcherry. Roi Tan cigars. Sail Aromatic.

No Good (handwritten)

52—American Broadcasting Companies, Inc., Chrm. Leonard H. Goldenson, 1330 Avenue of the Americas, New York, NY 10019, Phone 212-887-7777. **PRODUCTS:** ABC television network. Word Christian Book Publishers.

53—American Can Company, Chrm. B.S. Halsey, American Lane, Greenwich, CT 06830, Phone 203-552-2000. **PRODUCTS:** Aurora bathroom tissue. Bolt paper towels. Brawny paper towels. Dixie disposable cups and plates. Gala paper towels and napkins. Handy paper towels. Northern bathroom tissue and paper napkins.

54—American Cyanamid Company, Chrm. J.G. Affleck, Berdan Ave., Wayne, NJ 07470, Phone 201-831-2000. **PRODUCTS:** Blue Stratos cologne. Breck hair products. Centrum vitamins. Cie perfume. Clean Rinse hair rinse. Lady's Choice deodorant. Lasting Hold hair spray. Old Spice toiletries. Pierre Cardin toiletries. Pine-Sol cleaner. Spartus vitamins. Stresstabs vitamins.

56—American Express Company, Chrm. James D. Robinson, American Express Plaza, New York, NY 10004, Phone 212-480-2000. **PRODUCTS:** American Express card. Fireman's Fund insurance.

62—American Hoechst Corporation, Chrm. R. Sammet, Rt. 202-206 N., Somerville, NJ 08876, Phone 201-685-2000. **PRODUCTS:** Foster Grant sunglasses.

63—American Home Products, Chrm. J. W. Culligan, 685 3rd Ave., New York, NY 10017, Phone 212-878-5007. **PRODUCTS:** Advil arthritis medication. Aerowax. Anacin pain medication. Anbesol antiseptic. Arthritis Pain Formula medication. Beef-a-Roni. Beef-o-Getti. Bisodol mints. Black Flag insecticide. Brach's candy. Bronitin. Chef Boy-ar-dee food products. Compound W wart remover. Denalan denture cleaner. Dennison's chili. Denorex dandruff shampoo. Depend-O toilet cleaner. Diet Gard food supplement. Dristan decongestant. Dry & Clear medicated cleanser. Easy-Off oven cleaner. Easy-On starch. Freezone corn remover. Griffin shoe wax. Gumdinger candy. Heet liniment. HR carpet shampooing machines. Hula Chews coconut patties. Infrarub medication.

Jiffy-Pop popcorn. Momentum pain medication. Neet hair remover. Old English oil. Pam cooking spray lubricant. Preparation H hemorrhoid medication. Primatene asthma medication. Sani-Flush toilet cleaner. Sleep-Eze medication. 3-In-One oil. Wizard room deodorizer. Woolite laundry products. Youth Garde moisturizing cream.

64—American Honda Company, Director T. Sakema, Box 50, Gardena, CA 90247, Phone 213-327-8280. **PRODUCTS:** Honda motor vehicles.

66—American Tourister, Inc., Pres. Harvey Bomes, 91 Main St., Warren, RI 02885, Phone 401-245-2100. **PRODUCTS:** American Tourister luggage.

68—American Motors Corporation, Chrm. W. Paul Tippett, Jr., 27777 Franklin Rd., Southfield, MI 48034, Phone 313-827-1000. **PRODUCTS:** AMC automobiles. American Motors automobiles. Jeep automobiles. Renault automobiles.

79—American Telephone & Telegraph Company, Chrm. Charles Brown, 195 Broadway, New York, NY 10007, Phone 212-393-9800. **PRODUCTS:** A T & T phone services. Bell telecommunications products and services. Western Electric telephone equipment.

84—Amway Corporation, Chrm. Jay VanAndel, 7575 East Fulton Rd., Ada, MI 49344, Phone 616-676-6000. **PRODUCTS:** Amway household cleaning products and cosmetics.

87—Anderson Clayton Foods, Pres. F.F. Avery, P.O. Box 226165, Dallas, TX 75266, Phone 214-387-1224. **PRODUCTS:** Chiffon margarine. Igloo coolers. Seven Seas salad dressings.

88—Anheuser-Busch, Chrm. August A. Busch III, 721 Pestalozzi St., St. Louis, MO 63118, Phone 314-577-0577. **PRODUCTS:** Budweiser beer. Budweiser Light beer. Busch Bavarian beer. Michelob beer. Michelob Light beer. Natural Light beer.

99—Armstrong World Industries, Inc., Pres. Harry A. Jensen, P.O. Box 3001, Lancaster, PA 17604, Phone 717-397-0611. **PRODUCTS:** Armstrong carpets and tile.

103—Ashland Oil, Inc., Chrm. Orin E. Atkins, 1409 Winchester Ave., Ashland, KY 41101, Phone 606-329-3333. **PRODUCTS:** Valvoline motor oil.

104—Associated Coca-Cola, Chrm. C.S. Root, 320 Orange Ave., Daytona Beach, FL 32015, Phone 904-258-3355. **PRODUCTS:** Doric drink. Sunny Delight drink.

107—Associated Mills, Inc., Pres. Richard J. Stern, 111 N. Canal St., Chicago, IL 60606, Phone 312-454-5400. **PRODUCTS:** Pollenex Dial Massage showerheads.

111—Atlantic Richfield Company, Chrm. Robert O. Anderson, 515 S. Flower St., Los Angeles, CA 90071, Phone 213-486-3511. **PRODUCTS:** Arco petroleum products.

116—Avco Corporation, Chrm. Robert P. Bauman, 1275 King St., Greenwich, CT 06830, Phone 203-552-1800. **PRODUCTS:** Carte Blanche credit card. Paul Revere Life Insurance.

118—Avon Products, Inc., Chrm. David W. Mitchell, 9 W. 57th St., New York, NY 10019, Phone 212-546-6015. **PRODUCTS:** Avon cosmetics. Pizzazz makeup. Tiffany jewelry.

121—BMW of North America, Inc., Chrm. John A. Cook, Montvale, NJ 07645, Phone 201-573-2000. **PRODUCTS:** BMW automobiles.

127—Banfi Products, Chrm. Neil Trimble, 200 Sherwood Ave., Farmingdale, NY 11735, Phone 516-293-3500. **PRODUCTS:** Riunite wine.

129—Visa USA, Pres. Charles Russell, P.O. Box 8999, San Francisco, CA 94128, Phone 415-570-3200. **PRODUCTS:** VISA credit card.

137—Bausch & Lomb, Inc., Chrm. Daniel G. Schuman, 1 Lincoln First Square, Rochester, NY 14601, Phone 716-338-6000. **PRODUCTS:** Bausch & Lomb Softlens.

140—Beatrice Foods, Chrm. James L. Dutt, 2 N. LaSalle St., Chicago, IL 60602, Phone 312-782-3820. **PRODUCTS:** Cap 10 mineral water. Chuggers fruit juices. Clark Bar candy. La Choy dinners. Samsonite luggage. Shedd's Spreads. Swiss Miss pudding and frozen pudding bars. Tropicana orange juice.

142—Beecham Products, Pres. Robert Fallon, Box 1467, Pittsburgh, PA 15230, Phone 412-928-1000. **PRODUCTS:** Acu-test pregnancy test kit. Aqua Velva toiletries. Aqua-fresh toothpaste. Brylcreem hair products. Calgon bath products. Calgonite dishwashing detergent. Cling Free fabric softener. Dap home repair products. Femiron tablets. Geritol iron supplement. Hold cough medicine. Macleans toothpaste. Massengill douches. Nice cough lozenges. Popeye children's vitamins. Rose Milk skin care lotion. Sominex sleep aid. Sucrets lozenges. Vitabank vitamins. Vivarin stimulant tablets. Williams Lectric Shave lotion.

144—Beiersdorf, Incorporated, Pres. Peter Metzger, BDF Plaza, P.O. Box 5529, Norwalk, CT 06856, Phone 203-853-8008. **PRODUCTS:** Nivea skin cream and lotion.

150—Beneficial Corporation, Chrm. Finn M.W. Caspersen, 1100 Carr Rd., Wilmington, DE 19809, Phone 302-798-0800. **PRODUCTS:** Beneficial Finance Company. Beneficial Insurance. Beneficial National Bank. Western Auto stores.

159—Bic Pen Corporation, Chrm. Bruno Bich, One Wiley St., Milford, CT 06460, Phone 203-878-9341. **PRODUCTS:** Bic pens, lighters, and shavers.

166—Black & Decker, Chrm. Francis P. Lucier, 701 E. Joppa Road, Towson, MD 21204, Phone 301-828-3900. **PRODUCTS:** Black & Decker tools. McCulloch power saws.

169—H & R Block, Inc., Chrm. Henry Bloch, 4410 Main St., Kansas City, MO 64111, Phone 816-753-6900. **PRODUCTS:** H & R Block tax consultants.

170—Block Drug Company, Chrm. Leonard Block, 257 Cornelison Ave., Jersey City, NJ 07302, Phone 201-434-3000. **PRODUCTS:** All Clear decongestant. Aspercare aspirin. BC pain powder. Confident denture adhesive. Dentrol. Dentu-Creme denture cleaner. Dentu-Gel toothpaste. Dentu-Grip denture adhesive. Gentle Spring douche. Immerse hand lotion. Nytol sleeping pills. Poli-grip denture adhesive. Polident denture cleaner. Promise toothpaste. Shower Dew liquid soap. Smoker's Polident denture cleaner. Tegrin shampoo. Zestabs.

171—Blue Bell, Inc., Pres. L. K. Mann, P.O. Box 21488, Greensboro, NC 27420, Phone 919-373-3400. **PRODUCTS:** Jantzen clothing. Wrangler boots. Wrangler clothing.

175—Boise Cascade, Chrm. John Fery, One Jefferson Square, Boise, ID 83728, Phone 208-384-7560. **PRODUCTS:** Boise Cascade forest products.

179—Borden, Incorporated, Chrm. Eugene J. Sullivan, 277 Park Ave., New York, NY 10172, Phone 212-573-4000. **PRODUCTS:** Bama food products. Cracker Jack candy. Cremora non-dairy creamer. Eagle Brand condensed milk. Elmer's Glue. Kava coffee. Krylon paints. Pudding Bars. ReaLemon lemon juice. Wyler's beverages and soups.

188—Bristol-Myers Company, Chrm. Richard L. Gelb, 345 Park Ave., New York, NY 10022, Phone 212-546-4000. **PRODUCTS:** Assis-dent spray. Ban anti-perspirant. Beauty To Go haircare items. Behold polish. Body On Tap shampoo. Bromo Quinine. Bufferin pain medication. Clairol hair products. Comtrex cold medicine. Condition beauty pack. Condition shampoo. Congespirin cold medicine. Datril pain medication. Drano drain opener. Dry Ban anti-perspirant. Endust furniture spray. Excedrin pain medication. Feminique spray. Final Net hair spray. Fitch shampoo. Four-Way cold tablets. Herbal Essence shampoo. I Like My Grey shampoo. Kindness hair dryer. Kindness Soft Perm. Lady Clairol hair care products. Long & Silky hair conditioner. Loving Care hair care. Metrecal diet food. Miss Clairol hair products. Mr. Muscle oven cleaner. Mum deodorant. Naturally Blonde shampoo. Nice 'n Easy shampoo. No-Doz medication. Oven Guard. Plunge drain opener. Quiet Touch hair care. Renuzit freshener. Renuzit Fresh'n Dry air and fabric deodorizer. Sal Hepatica. Score hair care. Sea Breeze cream. Short & Sassy shampoo. Silence Is Golden cough syrup. Tickle deodorant. True Brunette hair dye. Twinkle metal polish. Ultra Ban anti-perspirant. Vanish toilet cleaner. Vitalis toiletries. Windex glass cleaner.

190—British Leyland Motors, Pres. Lord Stokes, 600 Willow Tree Rd., Leonia, NJ 07605, Phone 201-461-7300. **PRODUCTS:** Jaguar automobiles. MG automobiles. Triumph automobiles.

194—Brown-Forman Distributors, Chrm. R.S. Brown, Jr., Box 312, Harrods Creek, KY 40027, Phone 502-585-1100. **PRODUCTS:** Bolla wine. Cella wine.

195—Brown Group, Inc., Chrm. B.A. Bridgewater, Jr., P.O. Box 29, St. Louis, MO 63105, Phone 314-854-4000. **PRODUCTS:** Air Step shoes. Buskens shoes. Buster Brown shoes. Connie shoes. DeLiso shoes. Fanfares shoes. Footworks shoes. Levi's shoes and boots. Life Stride shoes. Marquiese shoes. Naturalizer shoes. Palter shoes. Regal shoes.

198—Brunswick Corporation, Chrm. K. Brook Abernathy One Brunswick Plaza, Skokie, IL 60077, Phone 312-470-4700. **PRODUCTS:** Brunswick sporting goods. Leisure Mart stores. Mariner outboard motors. Mercury outboard motors. Omega fishing reels. Zebco fishing reels.

204—Burlington Industries, Inc., Chrm. William A. Klopman, Box 21207, Greensboro, NC 27420, Phone 919-379-2000. **PRODUCTS:** Burlington corduroy. Burlington House sheets, draperies, and furniture. Burlington menswear. J.G. Furniture. Klopman fabrics.

205—Burmah-Castrol, Inc., Pres. M.J. Donahue, 401 Hackensack Ave., Hackensack, NJ 07601, Phone 201-488-1080. **PRODUCTS:** Castrol GTX motor oil.

206—Burris Industries, Inc., Chrm. J. Wayne Burris, P.O. Box 698, Lincolnton, NC 28092, Phone 704-735-0441. **PRODUCTS:** Burris Industries furniture.

207—Burroughs Corporation, Chrm. W. Michael Blumenthal, Burroughs Place, Detroit, MI 48232, Phone 313-972-7000. **PRODUCTS:** Burroughs computers and office machines. Memorex computers.

210—CBS, Inc., Chrm. Thomas H. Wyman, 51 W. 52nd St., New York, NY 10021, Phone 212-975-4320. **PRODUCTS:** CBS television network. Child Guidance toys. Columbia Records. Family Weekly magazine. Ideal toys. Missing Links game. Rubik's Cube. Tinkertoys.

211—CPC International, Chrm. James W. McKee, Jr., International Plaza, Englewood Cliffs, NJ 07632, Phone 201-894-4000. **PRODUCTS:** Best Foods food products. Golden Griddle syrup. Hellmann's mayonnaise. Karo syrup. Mazola vegetable oil and margarine. Niagara starch. S.B. Thomas' English Muffins. Skippy peanut butter.

217—Campbell Soup Company, Chrm. John T. Dorrance, Jr., Campbell Place, Camden, NJ 08101, Phone 609-964-4000. **PRODUCTS:** Annabelle's Fun & Foodrinkery-juice, Campbell's soups, juices, and canned foods. Comin' Home instant soup. Cup of Noodles. Farm Fresh mushrooms. Franco-American foods. Juice Works fruit drink. Le Menu frozen dinners.

Manhandler soups. Mrs. Paul's frozen foods. Pepperidge Farm foods. Prego spaghetti sauce. Swanson prepared foods. V-8 vegetable juice. Vlasic pickles.

219—Cannon Mills Company, Chrm. Otto G. Stolz, P.O. Box 107, Kannapolis, NC 28081, Phone 704-933-1221. **PRODUCTS:** Cannon towels and linens.

220—Canon USA, Chrm. Fujio Mitarai, One Canon Plaza, Lake Success, NY 11040, Phone 516-488-6700. **PRODUCTS:** Canon cameras and office machines.

227—Carnation Company, Chrm. H.E. Olson, 5045 Wilshire Blvd., Los Angeles, CA 90004, Phone 213-931-1911. **PRODUCTS:** Bright Eyes cat food. Buffet cat food. Carnation food products. Chef's Blend cat food. Coffee-Mate cream substitute. Come & Get It dog food. Fancy Feast cat food. Fish Ahoy. Friskies pet food. Instant Breakfast. Kitten Food. Little Friskies cat food. La Cantina Mexican-style cheese sauce. New Breed dog food. Mighty Dog pet food. Puppy Formula dog food. Trail Mix bars.

231—Carter Wallace, Chrm. Henry H. Hoyt, Jr., 767 5th Ave., New York, NY 10022, Phone 212-758-4500. **PRODUCTS:** Active tooth polish. Arid deodorant. Carter's Pills. Nair hair remover. Pearl Drops tooth polish. Rinse Away shampoo. Rise shaving cream. T-Zone cold remedy. Soft All Over body moisturizer.

233—Castle & Cooke, Inc., Pres. Ian R. Wilson, P.O. Box 2990, Honolulu, HI 96802, Phone 808-548-6611. **PRODUCTS:** Bumble Bee tuna and salmon. Bud of California fresh vegetables. Dole bananas, fresh mushrooms, and pineapple products.

247—Champion Spark Plug Company, Chrm. Robert A. Stranahan, Jr., P.O. Box 910, Toledo, OH 43661, Phone 419-535-2567. **PRODUCTS:** Anco wiper blades. Champion spark plugs.

250—Chattem, Incorporated, Chrm. Alex Guerry, 1715 W. 38th St., Chattanooga, TN 37409, Phone 615-821-4571. **PRODUCTS:** Pamprin medication tablets.

252—Chesebrough-Pond's, Chrm. Ralph E. Ward, Jr., 33 Benedict Place, Greenwich, CT 06830, Phone 203-661-2000. **PRODUCTS:** Aviance perfume. Aziza cosmetics. Bass shoes. Cachet perfume. Cachet Noir fragrance. Chimere perfume. Cutex nail polisher and remover. Health-Tex clothes. Night Musk fragrance. Pertussin cold medicine. Pizza Quick. Pond's skin creme. Pop Polish nail enamel. Premesyn tablets. Prince Matchabelli Toiletries. Prince tennis racquets. Q-tips. Ragú Italian foods. Rave hair care. Vaseline products. Wind Song perfume.

256—Chrysler Corporation, Chrm. L.A. Iacocca, 12000 Lynn Towsen Dr., Highland Park, MI 48231, Phone 313-956-5252. **PRODUCTS:** Chrysler automobiles. Dodge motor vehicles. Plymouth automobiles.

257—Church & Dwight Company, Pres. Dwight C. Minton, 20 Kingsbridge Rd., Piscataway, NJ 08854, Phone 201-885-1220. **PRODUCTS:** Arm & Hammer baking powder.

259—Airwick Industries, Inc., Pres. Michael J. Sheets, Commerce Rd., Carlstadt, NJ 07072, Phone 201-933-8200. **PRODUCTS:** Acutrim appetite suppressant. Airwand air freshener. Airwick air freshener. Binaca breath freshener. Carpet Fresh. Glamorene rug freshener. On Guard bowl cleaner. Plush carpet cleaner. Stick-Ups air freshener.

260—Citicorp, Chrm. Walter B. Wriston, 399 Park Ave., New York, NY 10043, Phone 212-559-1000. **PRODUCTS:** Diner's Club credit card.

264—City Investing Company, Chrm. George Scharffenberger, 59 Maiden Lane, New York, NY 10038, Phone 212-530-7300. **PRODUCTS:** Home Insurance Company.

267—The Clorox Company, Chrm. C.S. Hatch, 1221 Broadway, Oakland, CA 94612, Phone 415-271-7000. **PRODUCTS:** Clorox bleach. Clorox 2. Cream of Rice. Formula 409 cleaner. Fresh Scent liquid bleach. Fresh Step cat litter. Hidden Valley Ranch dressing. Kingsford charcoal. Kitchen Bouquet. Liquid Plumr drain opener. Litter Green cat litter. Matchlight charcoal. Soft Scrub cleanser. Tilex cleaner. Twice as Fresh deodorizer. Wave dry bleach.

269—The Coca Cola Company, Chrm. Roberto C. Goizueta, P.O. Drawer 1734, Atlanta, GA 30301, Phone 404-898-2121. **PRODUCTS:** Arista Records. Coca-Cola soft drink. Columbia movies and television productions. Five Alive fruit drink mix. Hi-C fruit drink. Maryland Club coffee. Minute Maid orange juice. Ramblin' Root Beer. Snow Crop juice. Sprite soft drink. Tab soft drink. Taylor wines. Vivante wines.

272—Coleco Industries, Inc., Chrm. Leonard Greenberg, 945 Asylum Ave., Hartford, CT 06105, Phone 203-278-

0280. **PRODUCTS:** Adam computer system. Coleco games. Coleco Vision. Donkey Kong video game. Pac Man Table Top Game. Smurf video cartridge. Zaxxon video game.

273—Coleman Company, Inc., Chrm. Sheldon Coleman, 250 N. St. Francis Ave., Wichita, KS 67201, Phone 316-261-3211. **PRODUCTS:** Coleman camping equipment.

274—Colgate Palmolive Company, Chrm. Keith Crane, 300 Park Ave., New York, NY 10022, Phone 212-310-2640. **PRODUCTS:** Ajax detergent. Cashmere Bouquet soap. Cold Power detergent. Colgate toothpaste. Crystal Clear detergent. Crystal White detergent. Curad bandages. Dermassage lotion. Dynamo detergent. Fab detergent. Fluorigard mouthwash. Fresh Start detergent. Irish Spring soap. Palmolive soap and detergent. Rapid-Shave shaving cream. Splendor shampoo. Super Suds soap. Ultra Brite toothpaste. Vel detergent. Wash 'n Dri disposable towels. Wildroot hair dressing.

275—S.R.L., Inc., CEO Thomas Gregory, 5400 Alla Rd., Los Angeles, CA 90066, Phone 213-827-2300. **PRODUCTS:** Sizzler restaurants.

278—Combe Incorporated, Chrm. Ivan D. Combe, 1101 Westchester Ave., White Plains, NY 10604, Phone 914-694-5454. **PRODUCTS:** Grecian Formula 16. Johnson's foot products. Lanacane skin medication. Lanacort. Odor Eaters. Vagisil lotion.

279—National Federation of Coffee Growers of Colombia, Chrm. Bernardo Rueda, 140 E. 57th St., New York, NY 10022, Phone 212-421-8300. **PRODUCTS:** Colombian coffee.

284—Congoleum Corporation, Chrm. Byron C. Radaker, 600 State St., Portsmouth, NH 03801, Phone 603-431-3131. **PRODUCTS:** Congoleum floor covering.

285—CIGNA Corporation, Pres. Robert D. Kilpatrick, 1185 Avenue of the Americas, New York, NY 10036, Phone 212-819-2500. **PRODUCTS:** Connecticut General insurance.

287—Consolidated Foods Corporation, Chrm. John H. Bryan, Jr., 3 First National Plaza, Chicago, IL 60602, Phone 312-726-2600. **PRODUCTS:** Aris gloves and knitted accessories. B&G pickles, relishes, and sauerkraut. Bali women's intimate apparel. Big Time candy. Booth fish and seafood products. Bryan meat products. Butternut candy. C&C soft drinks. Capri Sun fruit drinks. Chef Pierre frozen pies. Creamsicle frozen confections. Cruz Verde personal care and household products. Dici women's intimate apparel. Dreamsicle frozen confections. Douwe Egberts coffee, tea, and tobacco products. Electrolux vacuum cleaners and floor polishers. Fuller brushes and cleaning accessories. Fudgsicle frozen confections. Gallo meats. Gaviota ladies' swimswear. Good 'n Puddin frozen confections. Hanes hosiery and underwear. Hanes Too! hosiery. Hi-Brand meats. Hillshire Farm foods. Hollywood candy. Intradel personal care and household products. Isotoner gloves and knitted accessories. Jonker Fris fruits and vegetables. Kahn's meats. Lawsons convenience stores and food products. L'eggs hosiery. L'erin cosmetics. Lyon's restaurants. Milk Shake candy. Miss Den cosmetics and personal care products. Moccomat food service coffee and beverage systems. New Eyes eye makeup remover. Oxford chemicals. Payday candy. Popsicle frozen confections. PYA/Monarch food service distribution. Rudy's Farm meats. RusEttes frozen potatoes. Sara Lee frozen baked goods.

Sav-A-Stop service merchandising. Shasta soft drinks. Sheer Elegance hosiery. Sheer Energy hosiery. Showtoons boys' underwear. Sirena ladies' swimwear. Slenderalls hosiery. Smoky Hollow meats. Superior food service coffee and tea. Today's Girl hosiery. True Reflections pantyhose. Tyco toys. Underalls ladies' hosiery. Union refined sugar. WonderBra intimate apparel. Zero candy.

292—The Continental Corporation, Pres. John P. Mascotte, 180 Maiden Lane, New York, NY 10038, Phone 212-440-3000. **PRODUCTS:** Continental Insurance.

302—Cooper Laboratories, Chrm. Parker G. Montgomery, 3145 Porter Dr., Palo Alto, CA 94304, Phone 415-856-5000. **PRODUCTS:** Aveeno skin cleanser. Oral-B Zendium toothpaste. Permalens.

304—Corning Glass Works, Chrm. Amory Houghton, Jr., Houghton Park, Corning, NY 14831, Phone 607-974-9000. **PRODUCTS:** Chameleon sunglasses. Corelle dinnerware. Corning Ware dishes. Serengeti sunglasses. Sun Sensor sunglasses.

306—Cosmair, Inc., Chrm. Jacques H. Correze, 530 5th Ave., New York, NY 10036, Phone 201-382-7000. **PRODUCTS:** L'Oreal hair care products. Preference hair dye.

307—Cotter & Company, Chrm. John M. Cotter, 2740-52 N. Clyborne Ave., Chicago, IL 60614, Phone 312-975-2700. **PRODUCTS:** Tru-Value hardware stores.

321—Culbro Corporation, Chrm. Edgar M. Cullman, 605 3rd Ave., New York, NY 10158, Phone 212-687-7575.

PRODUCTS: Bachman Pretzels. Cains Marcelle potato chips. Chesty potato chips. Ex-Lax laxative. Gas X. Golden Crisp potato chips. Golden popcorn. Golden Ridges potato chips. Jax Cheese Twists snack food. KAS potato chips. Kitty Clover potato chips. Tor-Ticos tortilla chips. Viva corn chips. **TOBACCO PRODUCTS:** Brandee tobacco. Corina cigars. Greenbrier tobacco. Kentucky Club tobacco. London Dock tobacco. Robert Burns cigars. Royal Danish tobacco. Shakespeare cigars. Tijuana Smalls cigars. Tiparillo cigars. Tops Sweet tobacco. Van Dyck tobacco. Viking tobacco. Whitehall tobacco. White Owl cigars. William Penn cigars.

326—Agway, Inc., Chrm. George Steele, P.O. Box 4933, DeWitt, NY 13214, Phone 315-477-7061. **PRODUCTS:** Brooks chili hot beans. Brooks tangy catsup. Comstock Lite pie filling. Magic Blend dressing. Nallys chili products. Super Pop popcorn. Thank You puddings. Three Minute oats.

327—The Mathes Company, Chrm. Burke Mathes, P.O. Box 151, Athens, TX 75751, Phone 214-675-2291. **PRODUCTS:** Curtis Mathes televisions.

330—DPF, Inc., Chrm. Bertram J. Cohn, 141 Central Park Ave. S., Hartsdale, NY 10530, Phone 914-428-5000. **PRODUCTS:** Dolly Madison cakes and pies.

334—Dana Perfumes Corporation, Pres. Eugene J. Milano, 609 5th Ave., New York, NY 10017, Phone 212-751-3700. **PRODUCTS:** Canoe perfume. Tabu perfume.

337—Dart & Kraft, Inc., Chrm. John M. Richman, 2211 Sanders Rd., Northbrook, IL 60062, Phone 312-498-8000. **PRODUCTS:** Anova Master System. Breyers ice cream.

Durabeam flashlight. Duracell batteries. KitchenAid appliances. Kraft food products. Miracle margarine. Miracle Whip spread. Parkay margarine. Polar Caps ice cream and cookie sandwiches. Tupperware plastic containers. Velveeta cheese.

342—De Beers Consolidated Mines, Ltd., Chrm. H. F. Oppenheimer, 1345 Avenue of the Americas, New York, NY 10105, Phone 212-708-5000. **PRODUCTS:** De Beers diamonds.

344—Del Laboratories, Inc., Chrm. Martin Revson, 565 Broad Hollow Rd., Farmingdale, NY 11735, Phone 516-293-7070. **PRODUCTS:** Nutri-tonic shampoo. Sally Hansen's Hard-as-Nails.

347—Denny's, Inc., Chrm. Verne H. Winchell, 14256 E. Firestone Blvd., La Mirada, CA 90638, Phone 714-739-8100. **PRODUCTS:** Denny's restaurants. Winchell's Donut Houses.

357—Dr Pepper Company, CEO T.L. Kalahar, Box 225086, Dallas, TX 75265, Phone 214-824-0331. **PRODUCTS:** Canada Dry soft drinks. Dr Pepper soft drink. Seltzerbrate salt free seltzer. Welch's soft drink.

360—The Dow Chemical Company, Pres. Paul F. Oreffice, 2030 Dow Center, Midland, MI 48640, Phone 517-636-1000. **PRODUCTS:** Dow cleaner. Dowgard coolant. Handi-Wrap plastic products. Novahistine. Resolve cold gel. Saran Wrap plastic wrap. Ziploc bags.

369—E.I. Dupont de Nemours, Chrm. Irving S. Shapiro, 1007 Market St., Wilmington, DE 19898, Phone 302-774-

1000. **PRODUCTS:** Conoco gasoline. Dupont products. Lucite paint. Mutual Benefit Life insurance. Zerex antifreeze.

372—Dunkin' Donuts, Chrm. William Rosenberg, P.O. Box 317, Randolph, MA 02368, Phone 617-961-4000. **PRODUCTS:** Dunkin' Donuts.

377—Eastern Airlines, Inc., Chrm. Frank Borman, Miami International Airport, Miami, FL 33148, Phone 305-873-2211. **PRODUCTS:** Eastern Airlines.

379—Eastman Kodak Company, Chrm. Colby Chandler, 343 State St., Rochester, NY 14650, Phone 716-724-4000. **PRODUCTS:** Kodak photo products and services.

383—Economics Laboratory, Inc., Chrm. Pierson M. Grieve, Jr., Osborn Building, St. Paul, MN 55102, Phone 612-293-2233. **PRODUCTS:** Electrasol detergent. Free N' Soft fabric softener.

386—ERA Real Estate, Chrm. James A. Jackson, 4900 College Blvd., Shawnee Mission, KS 66201, Phone 913-341-8400. **PRODUCTS:** ERA Real Estate.

391—Emery Air Freight Corporation, Chrm. John C. Emery, Jr., Old Danbury Rd., Wilton, CT 06897, Phone 203-762-8601. **PRODUCTS:** Emery Air Freight.

393—Employers Insurance of Wausau, Chrm. T.A. Duckworth, 2000 Westwood Dr., Wausau, WI 54401, Phone 715-845-5211. **PRODUCTS:** Employers Insurance of Wausau. Wausau insurance.

399—Esmark, Inc., Chairman Donald P. Kelly, 55 E. Monroe St., Chicago, IL 60603, Phone 312-431-3600. **PRODUCTS:** Allsweet margarine. Aquarius perfume. Avis car rentals. Blue Plate foods. Brown 'n Serve sausage. Butterball turkeys. Colors to Go Makeup compact. Cross Your Heart bra. Danskin bras and panties. Epris perfume. Free Spirit bras. Hunt tomato products. Hunt-Wesson foods. Jensen stereo equipment. Jhirmack products. le Jardin de Max Factor fragrances. Max Factor cosmetics. Maxi by Max Factor. Missoni fragrance. Orville Redenbacher's popping corn. Peter Pan peanut butter. Playtex garments. Playtop undergarments. Round-the-Clock hosiery. Self-Defense moisturizer. Sizzlean bacon. Soup Starter. STP auto products. Sunlit sunflower oil. Swift's meats and meat products. Tampons feminine hygiene products. Tek toothbrush. Treasure Cove salad dressing. Wesson vegetable oil.

405—Exxon Corporation, Chrm. C.C. Garvin, Jr., 1251 Avenue of the Americas, New York, NY 10020, Phone 212-398-3000. **PRODUCTS:** Exxon petroleum products. Uniflo motor oil.

408—Faberge, Inc., Chrm. George Barrie, 1345 Avenue of the Americas, New York, NY 10019, Phone 212-581-3500. **PRODUCTS:** Aphrodesia perfume. Aqua Net hair spray. Babe cosmetics. Brut toiletries. Faberge cologne. Organics shampoo and conditioner. Tigress cologne. Touch of Class cologne. Turbo men's fragrance.

413—Falstaff Brewing Corporation, Chrm. Paul Kalmanovitz, 21 Tamal Vista Blvd., Corte Madera, CA 94925, Phone 415-924-7029. **PRODUCTS:** Falstaff beer.

422—Federal Express Corporation, Chrm. Frederick W. Smith, P.O. Box 727, Memphis, TN 38194, Phone 901-369-3600. **PRODUCTS:** Federal Express package service.

428—Fiat Motors of North America, Inc., Chrm. Antonio D'Emilio, 777 Terrace Ave., Hasbrouck Hgts., NJ 07604, Phone 201-393-4000. **PRODUCTS:** Ferrari automobiles. Fiat automobiles.

436—Firestone Tire & Rubber Company, Chrm. John J. Nevin, 6275 Eastland Rd., Brook Park, OH 44142, Phone 216-379-7000. **PRODUCTS:** Dayton tires. Firestone tires and automotive service.

443 —C.B. Fleet Company Inc., Chrm. Edward T. Hapgood, 1619 Wigginton Rd., Lynchburg, VA 24502, Phone 804-528-4000. **PRODUCTS:** Summer's Eve douche.

446—Florida Department of Citrus, Chrm. W. Bernard Lester, P.O. Box 148, Lakeland, FL 33802, Phone 813-682-0171. **PRODUCTS:** Florida orange juice. Orange juice from Florida.

448—Florists' Transworld Delivery Assn. (FTD), C.E.O. William A. Maas, P.O. Box 2227, Southfield, MI 48037, Phone 313-355-9300. **PRODUCTS:** FTD floral products by wire.

451—Ford Motor Company, Chrm. Philip Caldwell, The American Road, Dearborn, MI 48121, Phone 313-322-3000. **PRODUCTS:** Ford motor vehicles. Lincoln Continental automobiles. Mercury automobiles. Motorcraft automotive parts.

452—Foremost-McKesson, Inc., Chrm. Neil E. Harlan, One Post St., San Francisco, CA 94104, Phone 415-983-8300. **PRODUCTS:** Alhambra bottled water. Armor All car protection. Foremost dairy products. Valu-Rite drug stores.

454—Fotomat Corporation, Chrm. Richard Irwin, 64 Danbury Rd., Wilton, CT 06897, Phone 203-762-8621. **PRODUCTS:** Fotomat photographic service.

459—Reckitt & Colman North American, Inc., CEO Robert T. Silkett, One Mustard St., Rochester, NY 14692, Phone 716-546-3520. **PRODUCTS:** French's food products. Vive la Dijon mustard.

468—E & J Gallo, Chrm. Ernest Gallo, Box 1130, Modesto, CA 95353, Phone 209-521-3111. **PRODUCTS:** Andre champagne. Andre Spumanti wine. Andre Brut champagne. Carlo Rossi wine. French Columbard wine. Gallo wines. Polo Brindisi wine. Spanada wine.

478—General Electric, Chrm. John F. Welch, Jr., 3135 Easton Ave., Fairfield, CT 06431, Phone 203-373-2211. **PRODUCTS:** Advantage Series electronic telephones. General Electric (GE) products. Home Sentry smoke alarm. Hotpoint appliances.

479—General Foods, Chrm. J.L. Ferguson, 250 N. St., White Plains, NY 10625, Phone 914-683-2500. **PRODUCTS:** Alpha Bits cereal. Awake juice. Baker's chocolate. Batter'n Bake cooking mix. Birds Eye foods. Brim coffee. Cafe Francaise coffee. Cafe Vienna coffee. Calumet baking powder. Cocoa Pebbles cereal. Cool Whip whipped cream. Country Time lemonade. Crispy Critters cereal. Crispy Seasons. Cycle dog food. Dover Farms whipped topping. Dream Whip whipped cream substitute. Frosted Rice cereal. Fruit 'n Fibre cereal. Fruity Pebbles cereal. Gaines pet foods. General Foods International Coffees. Good Seasons salad dressing. Grape-Nuts cereal. Gravy Train pet food. Great Loaf meatloaf mix. Hale & Hearty dog food. Honey-Comb cereal. Jell-O desserts. Jell-O fruit and cream bars. Kool-Aid soft drink. Log Cabin syrup. Louis Rich meats. Max-pax coffee. Maxim coffee. Maxwell House coffee. Mellow Roast coffee. Minute Rice. Orange Plus orange juice. Oscar Mayer meats. Oven Fry. Pebbles cereal. Post cereals. Postum cereal. Prime dog food. Sanka coffee. Shake 'n Bake meat coating mix. Smurf-Berry Crunch cereal. Stove Top stuffing mix. Sugar Crisp cereal. Suisse Mocha coffee. Super Sugar Crisp cereal. Tang orange drink. Top Choice pet food. Yuban coffee.

482—General Mills, Inc., Chrm. H. Brewster Atwater, Jr., P.O. Box 1113, Minneapolis, MN 55440, Phone 612-540-3960. **PRODUCTS:** Baby Alive toys. Bake-a-Bar granola bar mix. Betty Crocker mixes. Bisquick mix. Body Buddies. Boggle game. Buc Wheats cereal. Care Bears toys. Cheerios cereal. Cocoa Puffs cereal. Crispy Wheat & Raisins. Fruit Roll-Ups. Gold Medal flour. Golden Grahams cereal. Granola bars. Hamburger Helper mix. Kaboom cereal. Kenner toys. Kix cereal. Lucky Charms cereal. Merlin game. Nature Valley Fruit Squeez juices. Nature Valley granola bars. Nerf toys. Nuts About Fruit bars. Parker Brothers games. Red Lobster restaurants. Saluto Deep Dish Pizza. Ship 'n' Shore clothing. Strawberry Shortcake cereal. Total cereal. Trix cereal. Wheaties cereal. Yoplait yogurt.

484—General Motors Corporation, Chrm. Roger B. Smith, General Motors Building, Detroit, MI 48202, Phone 313-556-

5000. **PRODUCTS:** AC-Delco auto parts. Buick automobiles. Cadillac automobiles. Chevrolet automobiles. General Motors parts. Mr. Goodwrench service. Oldsmobile automobiles. Pontiac automobiles.

487—GTE Corporation, Chrm. Theodore F. Brophy, One Stamford Forum, Stamford, CT 06904, Phone 203-357-2000. **PRODUCTS:** General Telephone & Electronics (GTE) products and services.

488—The General Tire & Rubber Company, Chrm. M. G. O'Neil, One General St., Akron, OH 44329, Phone 216-798-3000. **PRODUCTS:** General tires.

489—GENESCO, Inc., Chrm. John L. Hanigan, 111 Seventh Ave. N., Nashville, TN 37202, Phone 615-367-7000. **PRODUCTS:** Charm Step shoes. Dexter shoes. Jarman shoes. You Form It women's wear.

491—George A. Hormel & Company, Pres. Richard L. Knowlton, P.O. Box 800, Austin, MN 55912, Phone 507-437-5357. **PRODUCTS:** Hormel meats.

493—Georgia-Pacific, Chrm. Robert E. Floweree, 900 S.W. Fifth Ave., Suite 120, Portland, OR 97204. **PRODUCTS:** Coronet toilet tissue. Georgia-Pacific wood and paper products. Mister Big paper towels. Royal Oak charcoal.

494—Gerber Products Company, Chrm. Carl G. Smith, 445 State St., Fremont, MI 49412, Phone 616-928-2000. **PRODUCTS:** Gerber baby foods and products. Gerber Chunky foods. Onesies underwear.

495—Getty Oil Company, Chrm. Sidney R. Peterson, 3810 Wilshire Blvd., Los Angeles, CA 90010, Phone 213-381-7151. **PRODUCTS:** ESPN cable TV network. Getty Oil products.

498—The Gillette Company, Chrm. Colman Mockler, Jr., Prudential Tower Building, Boston, MA 02199, Phone 617-421-7000. **PRODUCTS:** Aapri apricot scrub. Adorn hair products. Atra razor. Bare Elegance. Brush-Up shaving brush. Cricket cigarette lighters. Daisy disposable shaver. Dippity-do hair gel. Dry Idea deodorant. Dry Look hair products. Earth Born shampoo. Eraser mate pens. Flair pens. For Oily Hair Only hair care. Gillette shavers and toiletries. Good News razor. Handler shampoo. Max hair dryer. Mink Difference shampoo. Mink hair spray. Paper Mate pens. Right Guard anti-perspirant. Silkience. Soft & Dri anti-perspirant. Supermax hair dryer. Tame hair products. Tony hair products. TracII shaving products. White Rain shampoo. Widget all-purpose tool.

507—Golden Grain Macaroni Company, Chrm. Paskey DeDomenico, 1111 139th Ave., San Leandro, CA 94578, Phone 415-357-8400. **PRODUCTS:** Golden Grain macaroni products.

509—B.F. Goodrich, Chrm. John D. Ong, 500 S. Main St., Akron, OH 44318, Phone 216-374-2000. **PRODUCTS:** B.F. Goodrich tires and stores.

510—The Goodyear Tire & Rubber Company, Chrm. Robert E. Mercer. 1144 E. Market St., Akron, OH 44316, Phone 216-794-2121. **PRODUCTS:** Goodyear tires.

512—W. R. Grace & Company, Chrm. J. Peter Grace, 1114 Avenue of the Americas, New York, NY 10036, Phone 212-764-5555. **PRODUCTS:** Bernstein salad dressing.

515—GrandMet USA, Inc., Chrm. Maxwell Joseph, 100 Paragon Dr., Mondale, NJ 07645, Phone 201-573-4000. **PRODUCTS:** Alpo pet food. Beef Bite Treats dog snack. Blue Lustre rug cleaner. Cream of Oats cereal. Demi-Tasse coffee cream liqueur. Red Man chewing tobacco.

521—Greyhound Corporation, Chrm. John Teets, Greyhound Tower, Phoenix, AZ 85077, Phone 602-248-4000. **PRODUCTS:** Armour meats. Bruce floor wax. Chiffon dishwashing soap. Dash dog food. Dial deodorant. Dial soap. Greyhound bus lines. LaSauce chicken sauce. Liqua 4 liquid soap. Peter Piper pizza restaurants. Tone soap.

526—Gulf Oil Corporation, Chrm. James E. Lee, 439 7th Ave., Pittsburgh, PA 15219, Phone 412-263-5000. **PRODUCTS:** Gulf petroleum products.

527—Gulf & Western, CEO Martin S. Davis, One Gulf & Western Plaza, New York, NY 10023, Phone 212-333-7000. **PRODUCTS:** Backwoods Smoker. Beach n' Beyond sportswear. Big A auto parts. Cameron fragrance. Catalina bathing suits and sportswear. Cheryl Tiegs sportswear. Cole of California sportswear. Cole Jrs. sportswear. Comfort Stride hosiery. Dutch Masters cigars. Easy To Be Me bra. El Producto cigars. Excello sportswear. Going Places sportswear. John Newcombe tennis wear. Kayser intimate apparel. Kurt Thomas Collection men's warmup suits. Liz Claiborne ladies' apparel. Madison Square Garden sports and entertainment organization. Mojud hosiery. Muriel cigars. No-Nonsense hosiery. Oscar de le Renta menswear. Paramount Pictures movies. Pascalle fragrance. Sandcastle sportswear. Silhouette Books. Simmons mattresses. Simon & Schuster publishers. Stetson western shirts and outerwear. Supp-hose stockings. Ultra Sense hosiery.

530—Haggar Company, Chrm. Edmond R. Haggar, 6113 Lemmon Ave., Dallas, TX 75209, Phone 214-352-8481. **PRODUCTS:** Haggar slacks.

532—Hallmark Cards, Inc., Pres. Donald J. Hall, 2501 McGee, Kansas City, MO 64108, Phone 816-274-5111. **PRODUCTS:** Hallmark cards.

539—Torstar Corporation, Chrm. Beland H. Honderich, One Yonge St., Toronto, Quebec, Canada, M5E 1P9. **PRODUCTS:** Harlequin books. Super Romance books.

545—Hartz Mountain Corporation, Chrm. Leonard N. Stern, 700 South 4th St., Harrison, NJ 07029, Phone 201-481-4800. **PRODUCTS:** Hartz Mountain pet supplies. 2 in 1 Plus Reflecting Collars.

546—Hasbro Industries, Inc., Chrm. Stephen Hassenfeld, 1027 Newport Ave., Pawtucket, RI 02862, Phone 401-726-4100. **PRODUCTS:** Hasbro toys.

552—G. Heileman Brewing Company, Inc., Chrm. Russell G. Cleary, 100 Harborview Plaza, La Crosse, WI 54601, Phone 608-785-1000. **PRODUCTS:** Blatz beer. Blitz Light beer. Old Style beer.

553—H.J. Heinz Company, Chrm. Henry J. Heinz II, P.O. Box 57, Pittsburgh, PA 15212, Phone 412-237-5757. **PRODUCTS:** Amore cat food. Crispy Crowns potatoes. Heinz food products. Mrs. Goodcookie cookies. Nine Lives cat food. Ore Ida potato products. StarKist canned tuna. Steak-Um. Weight Watchers foods and classes.

555—Helene Curtis Industries, Inc., Chrm. Gerald Gidwitz, 4401 W. North Ave., Chicago, IL 60639, Phone 312-661-0222. **PRODUCTS:** Arm in Arm anti-perspirant. Enden shampoo. Finesse hair conditioner. Suave shampoo.

556—Henry I. Siegel Co., Inc., President Jesse S. Siegel, 16 E. 34th St., New York, NY 10016, Phone 212-689-2323. **PRODUCTS:** Chic jeans. H.I.S. clothing.

558—Hershey Foods Corporation, Vice Chrm. William E. Dearden, 100 Mansion Rd. E., Hershey, PA 17033, Phone 717-534-4000. **PRODUCTS:** After Eight chocolate mints. Hershey's chocolate products. Kit Kat candy. Marabou milk chocolate roll. Mr. Goodbar candy. New Trail granola bars. Reese's candy. Rolo candy. Twizzlers candy. Whatchamacallit candy.

563—General Host Corporation, Chrm. Harris J. Ashton, 22 Gate House Rd., Stamford, CT 06902, Phone 203-357-9900. **PRODUCTS:** Hickory Farms of Ohio foods.

565—Hills Brothers Coffee, Chrm. Jose Luiz Zillo, P.O. Box 3149, San Francisco, CA 94119, Phone 415-546-4600. **PRODUCTS:** Hills Brothers coffee.

566—Hilton Hotels Corporation, Chrm. Barron Hilton, 9880 Wilshire Blvd., Beverly Hills, CA 90210, Phone 213-278-4321. **PRODUCTS:** Hilton hotel chain.

570—Holiday Inns Incorporated, Chrm. Roy Winegardner, 3742 Lamar Ave., Memphis, TN 38118, Phone 901-362-4001. **PRODUCTS:** Harrah's. Holiday Inn motels. Perkins restaurants.

572—Honeywell, Incorporated, Chrm. Edson W. Spencer, Honeywell Plaza, Minneapolis, MN 55408, Phone 612-870-5200. **PRODUCTS:** Honeywell computers. Honeywell smoke alarms.

574—Hoover Company, Chrm. Merle R. Rawson, 101 E. Maple St., North Canton, OH 44720, Phone 216-499-9200. **PRODUCTS:** Hoover electric floor cleaners. Hoover floor washers and polishers. Hoover vacuum cleaners. Hoover washing machines.

578—Houbigant, Inc., Chrm. Enrico Donati, 1135 Pleasantview Terrace, Ridgefield, NJ 07657, Phone 201-941-3400. **PRODUCTS:** April Showers perfume. Chantilly perfume. Houbigant perfume and cosmetics.

582—Household International, Inc., Chrm. Gilbert R. Ellis, 2700 Sanders Rd., Prospect Heights, IL 60070, Phone 312-564-5000. **PRODUCTS:** Household Finance loans. National car and truck rentals.

585—Huffy Corporation, Pres. Harry A. Shaw, III, 7701 Byers Rd., Miamisburg, OH 45342, Phone 513-866-6251. **PRODUCTS:** Huffy bicycles.

590—The E. F. Hutton Group, Inc., Chrm. Robert Fomon, One Battery Park Plaza, New York, NY 10004, Phone 212-742-5000. **PRODUCTS:** E. F. Hutton investments.

591—IC Industries, Chrm. William B. Johnson, One Illinois Center, Chicago, IL 60601, Phone 312-565-3000. **PRODUCTS:** Accent flavor enhancer. B&M Oven Baked beans. Dad's root beer. Downyflake breakfast food. Friend's oven baked beans. Heartland cereal. Laura Scudder's food products. Midas auto parts. Old El Paso Mexican foods. Pet Evaporated milk. Sego liquid diet meals. Top Ramen noodles. Underwood meat spreads. Whitman's chocolates.

593—IHOP Corporation, Chrm. Frederick Jahn, 6837 Lankershim Blvd., North Hollywood, CA 91605, Phone 213-982-2620. **PRODUCTS:** International House of Pancakes.

598—Hardee's Food Systems, Inc., Chrm. J. A. Laughery, 1233 N. Church St., Rocky Mount, NC 27801, Phone 919-977-2000. **PRODUCTS:** Burger Chef restaurants. Hardee's restaurants.

599—Rayovac Corporation, Pres. Thomas F. Pyle, 101 E. Washington Ave., Madison, WI 53703, Phone 608-252-7400. **PRODUCTS:** Ray-O-Vac batteries and lighting devices.

603—Howard Johnson Company, Chrm. Howard B. Johnson, One Howard Johnson Plaza, Dorchester, MA 02125, Phone 617-848-2350. **PRODUCTS:** Howard Johnson motels and restaurants.

604—MasterCard International, Inc., Pres. Russell E. Hogg, 888 7th Ave., New York, NY 10106, Phone 212-974-5700. **PRODUCTS:** MasterCard credit cards.

608—Insilco Corporation, Chrm. Durand B. Blatz, 1000 Research Pky., Meriden, CT 06450, Phone 203-634-2000. **PRODUCTS:** Red Devil paint.

611—International Business Machines, Chrm. John R. Opel, Old Orchard Rd., Armonk, NY 10504, Phone 914-765-1900. **PRODUCTS:** IBM information products. IBM office equipment.

619—International Telephone & Telegraph, Chrm. Rand Araskog, 320 Park Ave., New York, NY 10022, Phone 212-752-6000. **PRODUCTS:** Fresh Horizons bread. Home Pride bread. Hostess snack foods. ITT telephone and telegraph services. Scott's lawn products. Sheraton hotels. Wonder Bread.

627—Jack Eckerd Corporation, Chrm. Stewart Turley, P.O. Box 4689, Clearwater, FL 33518, Phone 813-397-7461. **PRODUCTS:** Eckerd Drugs. JByrons Department Stores.

634—Jeffrey Martin, Inc., Pres. Martin Himmel, 410 Clermont Terrace, Union, NJ 07083, Phone 201-687-4000. **PRODUCTS:** Ayds reducing help. Bantron. Colorex hair dye. Cuticura soap. Doans Pills. Porcelana cream. Pursettes premenstrual relief tablets. Pursettes tampons. Topol smokers toothpolish.

635—Jeno's, Inc., Chrm. Michael Paulucci, Box 6509, Duluth, MN 55802, Phone 218-723-5555. **PRODUCTS:** Colombo's frozen pizza. Jeno's frozen pizza. Natural Pizza.

643—John Hancock Mutual Life Insurance Co., Chrm. John G. McElwee, P.O. Box 111, Boston, MA 02117, Phone 617-421-6000. **PRODUCTS:** John Hancock Insurance.

646—S.C. Johnson & Sons, Inc., Chrm. Samuel C. Johnson, 1525 Howe St., Racine, WI 53403, Phone 519-756-7900. **PRODUCTS:** Agree shampoo. Bravo wax. Brite floor wax. Carnu polish. Clean & Clear wax. Edge shaving cream. Enhance perfume. Eureka! tents. Favor polish. Future floor coating. Glade room odorizer. Glade Spinfresh toilet-tissue roller. Glo Coat floor coating. Glory rug cleaner. J-Wax. Johnson wax. Klear floor coating. Off insect repellent. Pledge wax. Pride wax. Raid insecticide. Rain Barrel fabric softener. Shout stain remover. Soft Sense lotion. Step Saver cleaner.

648—Johnson & Johnson, Chrm. J.E. Burke, 501 George St., New Brunswick, NJ 08903, Phone 201-524-0400. **PRODUCTS:** ACT dental rinse-mouthwash. Band-Aid adhesive bandages. Carefree panty shields. Coldmax cold remedy. CoTylenol pain relief. Johnson's baby products. Micatin foot spray. No More Tangles. O. B. tampons. Reach toothbrush. Shower to Shower body powder. Sine-Aid sinus medication. Stayfree pads. Sure & Natural sanitary napkins. Take-Off makeup remover towels. Tricot Mesh Band-Aids. Tylenol pain medicine.

649—Johnson Products Company, Pres. George E. Johnson, 8522 S. LaFayette Ave., Chicago, IL 60620, Phone 312-483-4100. **PRODUCTS:** Afro Sheen hair care products. Black Tie cologne. Gentle Treatment hair relaxer. Ultra Sheen hair products.

650—Jones Dairy Farm, Chrw. Elizabeth J. Chisholm, P.O. Box 28, Atkinson, WI 53538, Phone 414-563-2431. **PRODUCTS:** Jones Farm pork sausage.

651—The Stroh Brewery Company, Chrm. Peter W. Stroh, One Stroh Drive, Detroit, MI 48226, Phone 313-446-2000.

PRODUCTS: Erlanger beer. Goebel beer. Old Milwaukee beer. Old Milwaukee Light beer. Piels beer. Piels Light & Draft Style beer. Primo beer. Schaefer beer. Schaefer Light beer. Schlitz beer. Schlitz Light beer. Schlitz Malt Liquor beer. Signature beer. Stroh's beer. Stroh's Light beer.

655—K mart Corporation, Chrm. Bernard M. Fauber, 3100 W. Big Beaver Rd., Troy, MI 48084, Phone 313-643-1000. **PRODUCTS:** K mart stores.

657—K-Tel International, Inc., Chrm. Philip Kives, 11311 K-Tel Dr., Minnetonka, MN 55343, Phone 612-932-4000. **PRODUCTS:** K-Tel records.

665—Keebler Company, Pres. Thomas M. Garvin, One Hollow Tree Lane, Elmhurst, IL 60126, Phone 312-833-2900. **PRODUCTS:** Chips Deluxe chocolate chip cookies. Fluffy cotton candy. Great Fruits chewy fruits. Harvest Wheats crackers. Ipso hard candies. Keebler cookies. Knots, Braids, & Nibs pretzels. Longfresh Thundermint chewing gum. Sportlife chewing gum. Town House crackers. Zesta crackers.

666—Kellogg Company, Chrm. William E. LaMothe, 235 Porter St., Battle Creek, MI 49016, Phone 616-966-2000. **PRODUCTS:** Apple Jacks cereal. Cocoa Krispies cereal. Corn Flakes cereal. Corny Snaps. Crispix party mix. Frosted Flakes cereal. Frosted Mini-Wheats cereal. Fruit Loops cereal. Kellogg's cereals. Kreemy cereal. Mini-Wheats cereal. Most cereal. Mrs. Smith's pies. Nutri-Grain cereal. Pop-Tarts. Product 19 cereal. Rice Krispies cereal. Special K cereal. Strawberry Krispies cereal. Sugar Pops cereal. Sugar Smacks cereal. Whitney's yogurt.

673—Kimberly Clark Corporation, Chrm. Darwin E. Smith, N. Lake St., Neenah, WI 54956, Phone 414-721-2000. **PRODUCTS:** Boutique bathroom tissue. Delsey bathroom tissue. Hi-Dri bathroom tissue. Hi-Dri household towels. Kleenex Huggies disposable diapers. Kleenex bathroom tissue. Kleenex facial tissue. Kleenex household towels. Kotex feminine pads and tampons. New Freedom feminine pads. Security tampons. Softique facial tissue. Super Dry disposable diapers.

689—La Maur, Inc., Chrm. Maurice L. Spiegel, 5601 E. River Rd., Minneapolis, MN 55440, Phone 612-571-1234. **PRODUCTS:** Style hair care products. Super Net hair spray. 24 Hour deodorant.

700—Lee Pharmaceuticals, Chrm. Dr. Henry L. Lee, Jr., 1444 Santa Anita Ave., South El Monte, CA 91733, Phone 213-442-3143. **PRODUCTS:** Faiance body cream. Resolution II diet tablets.

701—Lego Systems, Incorporated, Pres. John Sullivan, 555 Taylor Rd., Enfield, CT 06082, Phone 203-749-2291. **PRODUCTS:** Duplo Products pull toys and basic building sets. EXPERT BUILDER sets, accessory sets, and storage cases. LEGO building sets. LEGOLAND Town Sets. LEGO-LAND Space Sets.

705—Lennox Industries, Inc., Pres. John W. Norris, Jr., Box 809000, Dallas, TX 75380, Phone 214-783-5000. **PRODUCTS:** Lennox air conditioners.

708—Levi Strauss & Company, Chrm. Peter E. Haas, P. O. Box 7215 Levi's Plaza, San Francisco, CA 94120, Phone 415-544-6000. **PRODUCTS:** Levi's trousers.

713—Liberty Mutual Insurance Company, Chrm. Melvin B. Bradshaw, 175 Berkeley St., Boston, MA 02117, Phone 617-357-9500. **PRODUCTS:** Liberty Mutual Insurance.

717—Litton Industries, Chrm. Charles B. Thornton, 360 N. Crescent Dr., Beverly Hills, CA 90210, Phone 213-273-7860. **PRODUCTS:** Litton ovens.

721—Loews Corporation, Chrm. Laurence A. Tisch, 666 5th Ave., New York, NY 10019, Phone 212-409-2000. **PRODUCTS:** Accutron watches. Bulova watches. CNA Financial insurance. Loews theatres and hotels. **CIGARETTES:** Golden Lights. Kent. Max. Newport. Old Gold. Spring. Triumph. True. **TOBACCO PRODUCTS:** Bagpipe tobacco. Beech-Nut tobacco. Between-the-Acts tobacco. Big Red tobacco. Omega tobacco.

722—Jerrico, Inc., Chrm. Warren W. Rosenthal, P.O. Box 11988, Lexington, KY 40579, Phone 606-268-5211. **PRODUCTS:** Long John Silver's Seafood Shoppes.

732—Lumbermen's Mutual Casualty Company, Chrm. James S. Kemper, Jr., Kemper Building, Long Grove, IL 60049, Phone 312-540-2000. **PRODUCTS:** Kemper insurance.

735—MEM Company, Inc., Chrm. Stephen H. Mayer, Union St., Ext., Northvale, NJ 07647, Phone 201-767-0100. **PRODUCTS:** Cambridge cologne. English Leather toiletries. Essence of Musk women's fragrance. Heaven Sent all-over body spray. Wall Street men's fragrance.

742—Magic Chef, Inc., Pres. S. B. Rymer, Jr., 740 King Edward Ave., Cleveland, TN 37311, Phone 615-472-3371. **PRODUCTS:** Magic Chef appliances.

745—Emhart Corporation, Chrm. J. Mitchell Ford, P.O. Box 2730, Farmington, CT 06032, Phone 203-677-4631. **PRODUCTS:** Mallory batteries.

746—Savoy Industries, Inc., Chrm. Benson A. Selzer, 475 Park Ave. S., New York, NY 10016, Phone 212-889-6494. **PRODUCTS:** Empire toys. Hot cycle toys.

749—B. Manischewitz Co., Chrm. Bernard Manischewitz, 340 Henderson St., Jersey City, NJ 07302, Phone 201-333-3700. **PRODUCTS:** Manischewitz wines and foods.

754—Mars, Inc., Chrm. G. M. Conklin, 1651 Old Meadow Rd., McLean, VA 22102, Phone 703-821-4900. **PRODUCTS:** Cornquistos snacks. Crave cat food. Forever Yours candy. Kal Kan pet food. M & M's candy. Mars candy. Mealtime dog food. Milky Way candy. Royals mint chocolates. Snickers candy. Starburst candy. Stuff'n Such poultry stuffing. Summit cookie bars. Three Musketeers candy. Twix candy. Uncle Ben's rice.

759—Mary Kay Cosmetics, Inc., Chrm. Mary Kay Ash, 8787 Stemmons Freeway, Dallas, TX 75247, Phone 214-630-8787. **PRODUCTS:** Mary Kay cosmetics.

760—Masco Corporation, Chrm. Alex Manoogian, 21001 Van Born Rd., Taylor, MI 48180, Phone 313-274-7400. **PRODUCTS:** Delta faucets. Peerless faucets.

762—Masonite Corp., Chrm. Robert N. Rasmus, 29 North Wacker Dr., Chicago, IL 60606, Phone 312-372-5642. **PRODUCTS:** Masonite wood products.

765—Matsushita Electric of America, Chrm. M. Matsushita, One Panasonic Way, Secaucus, NJ 07094, Phone 201-348-

7000. **PRODUCTS:** Mr. Whisk wet/dry shaver. Motorola television. Panasonic televisions. Quasar television sets.

766—Mattel, Inc., Chrm. Arthur S. Spear, 5150 Rosecrans Ave., Hawthorne, CA 90250, Phone 213-978-5150. **PRODUCTS:** Intellevision games. M-Network video cartridge. Mattel Electronics. Mattel Toys. Vectrex video games.

768—Maytag Company, Chrm. Daniel J. Krumm, 807 S. 20th Ave. W., Newton, IA 50208, Phone 515-792-7000. **PRODUCTS:** Jenn Air appliances. Maytag appliances.

769—Mazda Motors of America, Pres. Kiyoshi Matsuno, 3040 E. Ana St., Compton, CA 90221, Phone 515-792-7000. **PRODUCTS:** Mazda automobiles.

770—McCormick and Co., Inc., Chrm. Harry K. Wells, 11350 McCormick Rd., Hunt Valley, MD 21031, Phone 301-667-7301. **PRODUCTS:** McCormick spices, condiments, and flavorings. Tio Sancho taco shells.

771—McDonald's Corporation, Chrm. Fred Turner, One McDonald's Plaza, Oak Brook, IL 60521, Phone 312-887-3200. **PRODUCTS:** McDonald's fast food.

777—The Mead Corporation, Chrm. B. R. Roberts, Courthouse Plaza, N.E., Dayton, OH 45463, Phone 513-222-6323. **PRODUCTS:** Mead school supplies.

778—Mego International, Inc., Chrm. Martin Abrams, 41 Madison Ave., New York, NY 10010, Phone 212-532-6333. **PRODUCTS:** Mego toys.

781—The Mennen Company, Chrm. L. Donald Horne, Hanover Ave., Morristown, NJ 07960, Phone 201-631-9000. **PRODUCTS:** Baby Magic shampoo. Balm Bar. Hawk cologne. Mennen after-shave. Millionaire cologne. Protein 21 shampoo. Protein 29 hair products. Skin Bracer toiletries. Smooth Legs shaving lotion. Speed-Stick deodorant.

782—Mentholatum Company, Pres. George H. Hyde, 1260 Niagara St., Buffalo, NY 14213, Phone 716-882-7660. **PRODUCTS:** Mentholatum.

783—Mercedes-Benz of North America, Inc., Pres. Werner F. Jessen, One Mercedes Dr., Montvale, NJ 07645, Phone 201-573-4600. **PRODUCTS:** Mercedes-Benz cars and buses.

785—Merle Norman Cosmetics, Inc., Chrm. J. B. Nethercutt, 9130 Bellanca Ave., Los Angeles, CA 90045, Phone 213-641-3000. **PRODUCTS:** Merle Norman cosmetics.

786—Merrill Lynch, Chrm. Roger E. Birk, 165 Broadway, New York, NY 10080, Phone 212-637-7455. **PRODUCTS:** Merrill Lynch investments.

790—Michelin Tire Corporation, Chrm. Paul Gorce, Box 1007, New York, NY 11042, Phone 516-488-3500. **PRODUCTS:** Michelin tires.

792—Miles Laboratories Incorporated, Chrm. Franz J. Geks, 1127 Myrtle St., Elkhart, IN 46515, Phone 219-264-8111. **PRODUCTS:** Alka-Seltzer. Alka-2. Bactine antiseptic. Bugs Bunny vitamins. Chocks vitamins. Copper-Kleen. Core C 500 vitamins. Flintstone's vitamins. One-A-Day vitamins. S.O.S. soap pads. Stressgard. Tuffy cleaning pads.

796—Milton Bradley Company, Chrm. James J. Shea, Jr., 1500 Main St., Springfield, MA 01101, Phone 413-525-6411. **PRODUCTS:** Bargain Hunter game. Battleship game. Big Track game. Connect Four game. Dark Tower electronic game. Double Track game. Hangman game. Life game. Micro-Vision game. Milton Bradley games. Numbers Up game. Operation game. Pivot pool game. Simon game. Staying Alive game. Stratego game. Super Simon game. Yahtzee game.

798—Minnesota Mining and Manufacturing, Chrm. L. W. Lehr, 3M Center, St. Paul, MN 55144, Phone 612-733-1110. **PRODUCTS:** Buf-Puf cleansing sponge. Rescue soap pads. Scotch Post-It note pads. Scotch tape. Scotchguard carpet cleaner. 3M products.

799—Minolta Corporation, Pres. Sam Kusmoto, 101 Williams Dr., Ramsey, NJ 07446, Phone 201-825-4000. **PRODUCTS:** Minolta cameras and office machines. Talker camera.

800—Minnetonka, Inc., Pres. Robert Taylor, Jonathan Industrial Center, Chaska, MN 55318, Phone 612-448-4181. **PRODUCTS:** Check-Up dentifrice. ShowerMate soap. Soft soap. Worksoap.

803—Mirro Company, Chrm. Charles W. Ziemer, 1412 Washington St., Manitowoc, WI 54220, Phone 414-684-4421. **PRODUCTS:** Mirro aluminum products.

806—Mobil Oil Corporation, Chrm. Rawleigh Warner, Jr., 150 E. 42nd St., New York, NY 10017, Phone 212-883-4242. **PRODUCTS:** Hefty trash bags. Jefferson Ward stores. Mobil oil products. Montgomery Ward stores. Steel Sak garbage bags.

815—Morton Thiokol, Incorporated, Chrm. Charles S. Locke, 110 Wacker Dr., Chicago, IL 60606, Phone 312-621-5200. **PRODUCTS:** Fantastik cleaner. Glass Plus cleaner. Grease Relief cleaner. Janitor-in-a-Drum. K2r spot remover. Morton salt. No-Pest Strip and liquid insecticides. Pine Power cleaner. Spray 'n Wash laundry product. Texize cleaner. Wood Plus furniture cleaner. Yes liquid laundry detergent.

831—Mutual of Omaha Insurance Company, Chrm. V. J. Skutt, Mutual of Omaha Plaza, Omaha, NE 68175, Phone 402-342-7600. **PRODUCTS:** Mutual of Omaha insurance.

832—Nabisco Brands, Chrm. Robert M. Schaeberle, 9 W. 57th St., New York, NY 10019, Phone 212-888-5100. **PRODUCTS:** Almost Home cookies. American Harvest crackers. Baby Ruth candy. Beech-Nut gum. Blue Bonnet margarine. Breath Savers. Bubble Gum chewing gum. Bugs Bunny cookies. Butcher Bones dog food. Butterfinger candy. Care-Free chewing gum. Charleston Chew candy. Chicken In a Biskit. Chips Ahoy cookies. Chit Chat crackers. Corn Champs snacks. Country Crackers. Cream of Wheat cereal. Duet fudge and peanut butter patties. Fig Newtons. Fleischmann's margarine. Junior Mints. Life Savers candy. Milk-Bone pet food. Musk after-shave. Nabisco foods. Oatmeal Fudge cookies. 100% Bran cereal. Oreo cookies. Planters peanuts. Potato 'n Sesame snack thins. Premium Saltines crackers. Replay gum. Ritz crackers. Royal pudding. Serutan tonic. Sesame crackers. Shredded Wheat cereal. Spoon Size cereal. Team cereal. Triscuit snack crackers. Wheat Thins crackers. Wheatsworth crackers.

833—Wilmar, Inc., Chrm. Fredrick F. Rohrer, Jr., 609 Epsilon Dr., Pittsburg, PA 15238, Phone 412-782-4666. **PRODUCTS:** NAPA auto parts.

842—National Distillers & Chemical Corporation, Chrm. Drummond C. Bell, 99 Park Ave., New York, NY 10016, Phone 212-949-5000. **PRODUCTS:** Almaden wine. Light Chablis wine.

843—National Enquirer, Chrm. Generoso Pope, 600 S.E. Coast Ave., Lantana, FL 33464, Phone 305-586-1111. **PRODUCTS:** National Enquirer tabloid newspaper.

849—National Presto Industries, Inc., Chrm. Melvin S. Cohen, 3925 N. Hastings Way, Eau Claire, WI 54701, Phone 714-839-2121. **PRODUCTS:** Presto appliances.

853—Dometic, Inc., Pres. Harry Eriksson, P.O. Box 2798, Bloomington, IL 61701, Phone 309-828-2367. **PRODUCTS:** Emerson televisions. Eureka vacuum cleaners.

855—Nationwide Insurance Company, Chrm. John E. Fisher, One Nationwide Plaza, Columbus, OH 43216, Phone 614-227-7111. **PRODUCTS:** Nationwide Insurance.

857—Nestle Company, Pres. David E. Guerrant, 100 Bloomingdale Rd., White Plains, NY 10605, Phone 914-682-6000. **PRODUCTS:** Beech-Nut Stages baby foods. Big Crunch candy. Chambourcy yogurt. Daybreak orange drink. Decaf coffee. Fresh 'n Lite salad dressing mix. Lean Cuisine low-cal foods. Libby's foods. Nescafe coffee. Nestea tea. Nestle's food products. Permasoft shampoo and conditioner. Quik drink mix. Simmer Soup. Souptime. Stouffer's frozen foods. Sunrise instant coffee. Taster's Choice coffee.

862—New York Life Insurance Company, Chrm. R. Manning Brown, Jr., 51 Madison Ave., New York, NY 10010, Phone 212-576-7000. **PRODUCTS:** New York Life Insurance.

868—Nissan Motors, Pres. T. Arakowa, Box 191, Gardena, CA 90247, Phone 213-532-3111. **PRODUCTS:** Datsun motor vehicles. Nissan motor vehicles.

869—Nissin Foods, Chrm. Akira Masumoto, 2001 W. Rosecram Ave., Gardena, CA 90249, Phone 213-321-6453. **PRODUCTS:** Hearty Cup O'Noodles.

873—North American Philips, Chrm. Pieter C. Vink, 100 E. 42nd St., New York, NY 10017, Phone 212-697-3600. **PRODUCTS:** Baker furniture. Chic personal care appliances. Genie door opener. LaserVision optical video-disc players. Magnavox television and audio-video centers. Norelco shavers and appliances. Odyssey video games. Omega band instruments. Philco televisions. Schick electric razors. Selmer band instruments. Sylvania televisions and audio-video centers. Trac Drive garage door openers. Wall Mount hair dryers.

874—North American Systems, Pres. Vincent Marotta, Box 46006, Bedford Heights, OH 44146, Phone 216-464-4000. **PRODUCTS:** Mr. Coffee coffeemaker.

876—InterNorth, Inc., CEO & Pres. Sam F. Segnar, 2223 Dodge St., Omaha, NE 68102, Phone 402-633-4000. **PRODUCTS:** Peak antifreeze.

877—Northland Aluminum Products, Inc., Pres. H. David Dalquist, Sr., Hwy 7 at Beltline, Minneapolis, MN 55416, Phone 612-920-2888. **PRODUCTS:** Nordic Ware.

879—Northwest Industries, Pres. Ben W. Heineman, 6300 Sears Tower, Chicago, IL 60606, Phone 312-876-7000. **PRODUCTS:** Acme boots. Fruit of the Loom underwear.

880—Northwestern Mutual Life Insurance Co., Chrm. Francis E. Ferguson, 720 E. Wisconsin Ave., Milwaukee, WI 53202, Phone 414-271-1444. **PRODUCTS:** Northwestern Mutual life and disability income insurance.

882—Muralo Company, Chrm. Ed Norton, Jr., 148 E. 5th St., Bayonne, NJ 07002, Phone 201-437-0770. **PRODUCTS:** Muralo paint and stain. Olympic paints.

884—Noxell Corporation, Chrm. G. Lloyd Bunting, Box 1799, Baltimore, MD 21203, Phone 301-628-7300. **PRODUCTS:** Cover Girl cosmetics. Marathon mascara. Moisture Wear makeup. Noxzema Continuous Protection cream. Noxzema skin cream. Raintree skin cream.

885—The O'Brien Corporation, Chrm. Jerome J. Crowley, 450 E. Grand Ave. S., San Francisco, CA 94080, Phone 415-761-2300. **PRODUCTS:** Fuller O'Brien paints.

887—Ocean Spray Cranberries, Chrm. Stuart Pedersen, Water St., Plymouth, MA 02360, Phone 617-747-1000. **PRODUCTS:** Firehouse Jubilee tomato cocktail. Ocean Spray cranberry products.

892—Olin Corporation, Chrm. J. M. Henske, 120 Long Ridge Rd., Stamford, CT 06904, Phone 203-356-2000. **PRODUCTS:** Olin H-T-H pool chemicals. Pace pool products.

896—Oneida Ltd. Silversmiths, Chrm. John L. Marcellus, Kenwood Station, Oneida, NY 13421, Phone 315-361-3000. **PRODUCTS:** Oneida silversmiths.

898—Olympus Camera Company, Chrm. Robert E. Brockway, 145 Crossway Park, Woodbury, NY 11797, Phone 516-364-3000. **PRODUCTS:** Olympus cameras.

905—Owens-Corning Fiberglas, Pres. Wm. W. Boeschenstein, Fiberglas Tower, Toledo, OH 43659, Phone 419-248-8000. **PRODUCTS:** Owens-Corning insulation.

907—Lanier Business Products, Inc., Chrm. Gene W. Milner, 1700 Chantilly Dr. NE, Atlanta, GA 30324, Phone 404-329-8000. **PRODUCTS:** Lanier business products.

910—Pabst Brewing Company, Pres. William F. Smith, Jr., 1000 N. Market St., Milwaukee, WI 53201, Phone 414-347-7555. **PRODUCTS:** Andeker beer. Buckhorn beer. Hamm's beer. Hamm's Special Light beer. Jacob Best Premium Light beer. Olde English 800 beer. Olympia beer. Olympia Gold beer. Pabst Blue Ribbon beer. Pabst Extra Light beer. Pabst Special Dark beer.

911—Paine, Webber, Inc., Chrm. Donald B. Marron, 140 Broadway, New York, NY 10005, Phone 212-437-2121. **PRODUCTS:** Paine-Webber brokers.

914—Pan American World Airways, Inc., Chrm. C. Edward Acker, 200 Park Ave., New York, NY 10166, Phone 212-880-1234. **PRODUCTS:** Pan American airways.

916—Papercraft Corporation, Chrm. Joseph M. Katz, Papercraft Park, Pittsburgh, PA 15238, Phone 412-362-8000. **PRODUCTS:** Tid-D-Bol toilet cleaner.

924—J.C. Penney, Chrm. Donald V. Seibert, 1301 Ave. of The Americas, New York, NY 10019, Phone 212-957-4321. **PRODUCTS:** J. C. Penney department stores. Penney's department stores.

926—Pennwalt Corporation, Chrm. Edwin E. Tuttle, 3 Parkway, Philadelphia, PA 19102, Phone 215-587-7000. **PRODUCTS:** Allerest allergy medication. Caldecort. Coldene medicine. Desenex athlete's foot medication. Sinarest decongestant.

927—Pennzoil Company, Chrm. J. Hugh Liedtke, P.O. Box 2967, Houston, TX 77001, Phone 713-236-7878. **PRODUCTS:** Pennzoil motor oil.

929—Peoples Energy Corporation, Chrm. Eugene A. Tracy, 122 S. Michigan Ave., Chicago, IL 60603, Phone 312-431-4200. **PRODUCTS:** Natural Gas fuel.

930—PepsiCo, Chrm. Donald M. Kendall, Anderson Hill Rd., Purchase, NY 10577, Phone 914-253-2000. **PRODUCTS:** Bacon Nips snacks. Chee-tos cheese puffs. Diet Pepsi soft drink. Doritos corn chips. Fritos snack foods. Grandma's cookies. Lay's potato chips. Mountain Dew soft drink. O'Gradys potato chips. Pepsi-Cola soft drink. Personal Pan Pizza. Pizza Hut restaurant. Ruffles potato chips. Ta-Tos potato chips. Taco Bell fast food. Tostitos tortilla chips. Wilson sporting goods.

933—Peter Paul Cadbury, Inc., Chrm. Robert E. Ix, New Haven Rd., Naugatuck, CT 06770, Phone 203-729-0221. **PRODUCTS:** Almond Joy candy. Cadbury candy. Cadbury Crisp. Caravelle candy. Mounds candy. Peter Paul candy. Schweppes soft drinks. Thick candy bar. York Peppermint Pattie candy.

937—Pfizer, Inc., Chrm. Henry L. Ross, Jr., 235 E. 42nd St., New York, NY 10017, Phone 212-573-2323. **PRODUCTS:** Barbasol shaving cream. Ben-Gay rub. Coty perfumes. Desitin skin products. Emeraude perfume. Hai Karate cologne. Nuance perfume. Shape 'n Shadow eye kit. Silk'n Satin. Sophia perfume. Stetson cologne. TZ-3 athlete's foot ointment. Unisom. Visine eye drops.

939—Philip Morris, Incorporated, Chrm. George Weissman, 100 Park Ave., New York, NY 10017, Phone 212-679-1800. **PRODUCTS:** Like caffeine-free cola. Lite beer. Lowenbrau beer. Miller beer. Mister Brau beer. Seven-Up soft drink. **CIGARETTES:** Alpine. Benson & Hedges. Cambridge. Marlboro. Merit. Multifilter. Parliament. Philip Morris. Players. Saratoga. Virginia Slims.

940—Phillips Petroleum, Chrm. Wm. C. Douce, 18 Phillips Building, Bartlesville, OK 74004, Phone 918-661-6600. **PRODUCTS:** Phillips petroleum products. TropArtic batteries and oil.

947—The Pillsbury Company, Chrm. William H. Spoor, Pillsbury Center, Minneapolis, MN 55402, Phone 612-330-4966. **PRODUCTS:** All Ready pie crust. Bennigan's restaurants. Bundt cakes. Burger King restaurants. Figurines. Frosting Supreme. Fudge Jumbles dessert mixes. Green Giant food products. Haagen-Dazs ice cream. Hungry Jack biscuits. Pillsbury mixes. Poppin Fresh dough. Spooners Soft Serve dairy dessert. Steak & Ale restaurants.

952—Pittway Corporation, Pres. Neison Harris, 333 Skokie Rd., Northbrook, IL 60062, Phone 312-498-1260. **PRODUCTS:** First Alert fire detector.

955—Polaroid Corporation, Pres. W.J. McCune, Jr., 549 Technology Sq., Lincoln, MA 01773, Phone 617-577-2000. **PRODUCTS:** Polaroid cameras.

965—Procter & Gamble, Chrm. Owen Butler, P.O. Box 599, Cincinnati, OH 45201, Phone 513-562-1100. **PRODUCTS:** Always minipads and maxipads. Banner toilet tissue. Biz bleach. Bold detergent. Bounce fabric softener. Bounty paper towels. Camay soap. Cascade detergent. Certain bathroom tissue. Charmin toilet tissue. Cheer detergent. Chloraseptic oral antiseptic and anesthetic. Cinch cleaner. Citrus Hill orange juice. Coast soap. Comet cleanser. Crest toothpaste. Crisco oil and shortening. Crush soft drink. Dash detergent. Dawn dish detergent. Downy fabric softener. Dreft detergent. Duncan Hines foods. Era detergent. Fluffo shortening. Folger's coffee. Gain detergent. Gleem toothpaste. Head & Chest cold remedy products. Head & Shoulders shampoo. High Point coffee. Hires soft drink. Ivory soap and detergent. Jif peanut butter. Joy detergent. Lava liquid soap. Lava soap. Luv's diapers. Merit towels. Mr. Clean cleaner. Necta Sweet saccharin. Norforms feminine hygiene products. Norwich aspirin. Norwich glycerin suppositories. NP-27 athlete's foot care. Oasis deodorant. Oxydol detergent. Pampers diapers. Pepto-Bismol. Pert shampoo. Prell shampoo. Pringle's potato chips. Puffs tissue. Puritan cooking oil. Rejoice liquid soap. Safeguard soap. Scope mouthwash. Secret deodorant. Solo liquid detergent. Spic and Span cleaner. Summit towels. Sun-drop soft drink. Sure anti-perspirant. Tender Leaf tea. Tide detergent. Top Job household cleaner. Unguentine first aid and sunburn products. Vibrant bleach. White Cloud tissue. Wondra hand lotion. Zest detergent bar.

966—Prudential Insurance, Chrm. Robert A. Beck, Prudential Plaza, Newark, NJ 07101, Phone 201-877-6000. **PRODUCTS:** Bache Group financial service. Prudential Insurance.

968—Publishers Clearing House, Pres. Robin Smith, 382 Channel Dr., Port Washington, NY 11050, Phone 516-883-5432. **PRODUCTS:** magazine subscriptions.

970—Purex Industries, Inc., Chrm. William R. Tincher, 5101 Clark Ave., Lakewood, CA 90712, Phone 213-634-3300. **PRODUCTS:** Bo Peep ammonia. Brillo soap pads. Dobie Pads. Dutch Cleanser. Instant Fels. Purex bleach. Purex detergent. Sta-Puf fabric softener. Sweet Heart bar soap. Toss N Soft fabric softener. Trend detergent.

971—Puritan Fashions Corporation, Chrm. Carl Rosen, 1400 Broadway, New York, NY 10018, Phone 212-575-0800. **PRODUCTS:** Calvin Klein clothing.

972—Purolator, Inc., Chrm. Nicholas F. Brady, 255 Old New Brunswick Rd., Piscataway, NJ 08854, Phone 201-885-1100. **PRODUCTS:** Purolator courier service. Purolator filters.

974—Quaker Oats Company, Chrm. William D. Smithburg, 345 Merchandise Mart, Chicago, IL 60654, Phone 312-222-7111. **PRODUCTS:** Aunt Jemima pancake mix. Cap'n Crunch cereal. Celeste Italian foods. Country Ladle Soup Fixings. Creamy Wheat cereal. Crunch Berries cereal. Fisher-Price toys. Gatorade soft drink. Grain Drops snacks. Halfsies low-sugar cereal. Harvest Crunch cereal. Ken-L-Ration pet food. Kibbles & Bits pet food. King Vitamin cereal. Life cereal. Puffed Wheat cereal. Puss 'n Boots cat food. Quaker cereals. Quaker chewy granola bars. Tender Chunks dog food.

975—Quaker State Oil, Chrm. T. A. Anderson, 255 Elm St., Oil City, PA 16301, Phone 814-536-7541. **PRODUCTS:** Quaker State motor oil.

978—Questor Corporation, Chrm. Dan W. Lufkin, P.O. Box 30101, Tampa, FL 33614, Phone 813-884-3531. **PRODUCTS:** Spaulding Top Flight golf balls.

980—RCA Corporation, Chrm. Thornton F. Bradshaw, 30 Rockefeller Plaza, New York, NY 10020, Phone 212-621-6000. **PRODUCTS:** Hertz car rentals. NBC television network. RCA television sets. **RECORD LABELS OWNED BY RCA**—BET-Bethlehem. DRG. ERO-Erato. FFL-Free Flight. FLD-Flying Dutchman. GDM-Gold Mind. GNT-Grunt. GRY-Gryphon. IAM-I & M. KDU-Kudu. MLN-Millennium. PAB-Pablo. PAN-Panorama. PNT-Planet. RDS-Roadshow. ROC-Rocket. SLR-Solar. SSL-Salsoul. TAT-Tattoo. VIC-Victor. VTR-Victrola. WDN-Wooden Nickel. WDS-Windsong.

982—Raleigh Industries of America, Inc., Chrm. R. A. L. Roberts, 1168 Commonwealth Ave., Boston, MA 02134, Phone 617-734-0240. **PRODUCTS:** Raleigh bicycles.

983—Ragold, Inc., Pres. Joerg Schindler, 500 N. Michigan #1700, Chicago, IL 60611, Phone 312-222-1888. **PRODUCTS:** Velamints breath mints.

984—Ralston Purina Company, Pres. William P. Stiritz, Checkerboard Sq., St. Louis, MO 63188, Phone 314-982-1000. **PRODUCTS:** Bonz dog snacks. Butcher's Blend dog food. Checkerboard foods. Chex cereal. Chicken-of-the-Sea tuna. Choice Morsels cat food. Chuck Wagon pet food. Cookie Crisp cereal. Dinky Donuts cereal. Donkey Kong cereal. Fit

& Trim dog food. Flavor Plus dog food. Good News cat food. Happy Cat "semidry" cat food. Hero dog food. Honey brand cereal. Jack-in-the-Box fast foods. Main Stay dog food. Meow Mix cat food. Praise dog food. Puppy Chow dog food. Purina pet food. Rice Chex cereal. Roverolli dog snack. Special Dinners pet food. Tender Vittles cat food. Thrive cat food. Wheat Chex cereal.

985—Ramada Inns, Inc., Chrm. Marion William Isbell, 3838 E. Van Buren, Phoenix, AZ 85008, Phone 602-273-4000. **PRODUCTS:** Ramada Inns motels.

991—Raytheon Company, Chrm. Thomas L. Phillips, 141 Spring St., Lexington, MA 02173, Phone 617-862-6600. **PRODUCTS:** Amana appliances.

1013—Revlon, Inc., Chrm. Michel C. Bergerac, 767 5th Ave., New York, NY 10153, Phone 212-572-5000. **PRODUCTS:** Albolene Cream. Aquamarine powder. Charlie perfume. Chaz cologne. Colorsilk hair dye. Esoterica lotion. Flex Balsam hair conditioner. Flex-Net hair spray. For Bodies Only liquid soap. Hydra-Curve contact lens. Intimate lotion. Jontue perfume. Mitchum anti-perspirant. Moon Drops lipstick. Natural Wonder cosmetics. No Salt flavoring. Ora Brite. Ora Fix denture adhesive. Revlon cosmetics. Scoundrel perfume. Top Brass hair products. Tums medication. Ultima II cosmetics.

1015—R.J. Reynolds Industries, Inc., CEO J. Tylee Wilson, World Headquarters Bldg., Winston-Salem, NC 27102, Phone 919-773-2000. **PRODUCTS:** A.1. Steak Sauce. Brer Rabbit molasses. Chun King oriental foods. College Inn food products. Colony wines. Coronation specialty foods. Davis baking powder. Del Monte foods. Grey Poupon Dijon mustard.

Harvey's Bristol Cream sherry. Hawaiian Punch fruit drink. Inglenook wines. Italian Swiss Colony wines. Kentucky Fried Chicken. Lancer's wine. Milk-Mate chocolate syrup. Morton's frozen foods. My-T-Fine pudding and pie filling. Ortega chiles. Patio Mexican foods. PortaTap boxed wine. Sea Land freight service. Vermont Maid maple syrup. **CIGARETTES:** Camel. Doral II. More. Now. Salem. Vantage. Winston. **TOBACCO PRODUCTS:** Carter Hall. Day's Work. George Washington. Madeira Gold. Prince Albert. Royal Comfort pipe tobacco. Work Horse chewing tobacco.

1016—Reynolds Metals, Chrm. David P. Reynolds, 6601 W. Broad St., Richmond, VA 23261, Phone 804-281-2000. **PRODUCTS:** Reynolds aluminum products.

1021—Richardson-Vicks, Inc., Chrm. H. Smith Richardson, Jr., Ten Westport Rd., Wilton, CT 06897, Phone 203-762-2222. **PRODUCTS:** Biactrin facial cleanser. Cepacol mouthwash and lozenges. Clearasil skin medication. Cremacoat cough medicine. Dismiss douches. Fasteeth denture adhesive. Formby's wood care products. Formula 44 cough medicine. Lavoris mouthwash. Lifestage vitamins. NyQuil decongestant. Oil of Olay lotion. Sassoon D dandruff shampoo. Sassoon D scalp and hair conditioner. Sinex. Surround cough syrup. Tempo antacid. Vaporub cough drops. Vicks medications. Vidal Sassoon hair products.

1025—Rival Manufacturing Company, Pres. I. H. Miller, 36th at Bennington, Kansas City, MO 64129, Phone 816-861-1000. **PRODUCTS:** Rival appliances.

1029—A. H. Robins Company, Inc., Chrm. E. C. Robins, 1407 Cummings Dr., Richmond, VA 23220, Phone 804-

257-2000. **PRODUCTS:** Chap Stick lip balm. Exelle lipstick. Extend 12 cough medicine. Face Quencher. Lip Quencher. Robitussin cough medicine. Sentry flea collars. Sergeant's pet supplies.

1030—Rockwell International Corporation, Chrm. Robert Anderson, 600 Grant St., Pittsburgh, PA 15219, Phone 412-565-7495. **PRODUCTS:** Rockwell tools.

1033—Rollins, Inc., Chrm. O. Wayne Rollins, P.O. Box 647, Atlanta, GA 30301, Phone 404-873-2355. **PRODUCTS:** Orkin Pest Control.

1040—Rothmans of Canada, Ltd., Chrm. C. Landmark, 1500 Don Mills Rd., Don Mills, Ontario, Canada M3B 3L1. **PRODUCTS:** Colt 45 malt liquor.

1043—Royal Crown Cola Company, Chrm. William T. Young, 41 Perimeter Ctr. East N.E., Atlanta, GA 30346, Phone 404-394-6120. **PRODUCTS:** Arby's restaurants. Diet-Rite soft drink. RC Cola soft drink.

1045—Rubbermaid, Inc., Chrm. Stanley C. Gault, 1147 Adron Rd., Wooster, OH 44691, Phone 216-264-6464. **PRODUCTS:** Rubbermaid products.

1049—Rust-Oleum Corporation, Pres. Rex Reade, 11 Hawthorn Pky., Vernon Hills, IL 60061, Phone 312-367-7700. **PRODUCTS:** Rust-Oleum rust preventive coating.

1050—Ryder System, Inc., Chrm. Leslie O. Barnes, 3600 N.W. 82nd Ave., Miami, FL 33166, Phone 305-593-3726. **PRODUCTS:** Ryder Truck Rental.

1051—S C M Corporation, Pres. Paul H. Elicker, 299 Park Ave., New York, NY 10017, Phone 212-752-2700. **PRODUCTS:** Glidden paint.

1055—Safeco Corporation, Chrm. R. M. Trafton, Safeco Plaza, Seattle, WA 98185, Phone 206-545-5000. **PRODUCTS:** Safeco Insurance.

1057—Saga Corporation, Chrm. Ernest C. Arbuckle, One Saga Lane, Menlo Park, CA 94025, Phone 415-854-5150. **PRODUCTS:** Straw Hat Pizza Palaces.

1058—St. Regis Paper Company, Chrm. William R. Haselton, 237 Park Ave., New York, NY 10017, Phone 212-808-6000. **PRODUCTS:** St. Regis paper products.

1059—Sambo's Restaurants, Chrm. Robert Luckey, 6400 Cindy Lane, Carpinteria, CA 93013, Phone 805-687-6777. **PRODUCTS:** Sambo's Restaurants.

1062—Sandoz, Inc., Chrm. Marc Moret, One Lafayette Place, Greenwich, CT 06830, Phone 203-622-0005. **PRODUCTS:** Ovaltine malt drink. Triaminic cough formula.

1067—Savin Corporation, Chrm. E. Paul Charlap, Columbus Ave., Valhalla, NY 10595, Phone 914-769-9500. **PRODUCTS:** Savin Corporation business machines.

1068—The Savings & Loan Foundation, Chrm. Tom B. Scott, Jr., 1522 K Street N.W. #910, Washington, DC 20005, Phone 202-842-4300. **PRODUCTS:** Savings and Loans Foundations.

1071—Schering-Plough Corporation, Pres. Robert P. Luciano, Galloping Hill Road, Kenilworth, NJ 07033, Phone 201-558-4000. **PRODUCTS:** Aftate. Artra cosmetics. Aspergum. Chooz gum. Coppertone suntan products. Coricidin cough medicine. Correctol laxative. Daydreams perfume. Derusto special paints. Di-Gel antacid. Dr. Scholl's foot products. Duration spray. Feen-a-mint laxative. For Faces Only sun protection. Fresh & Lovely lipstick. Great Lash mascara. Maybelline cosmetics. Mistol nasal drops. Paas Easter egg colors. QT sun tan lotion. Scholl foot powder. Scholl sandals. Solarcaine sunburn medication. St. Joseph aspirin. Sudden Tan lotion. Tropical Blend suntan lotion.

1078—Scott Paper Company, Pres. Philip E. Lippincott, Scott Plaza, Philadelphia, PA 19113, Phone 215-521-5000. **PRODUCTS:** Scotties facial tissue. ScotTowels paper towels. ScotTowels Junior paper towels. Soft'n' Pretty bath tissue. Viva paper towels.

1079—Scott's Liquid Gold, Inc., Pres. Jerome J. Goldstein, 4880 Havana St., Denver, CO 80239, Phone 303-373-4860. **PRODUCTS:** Aquafilter cigarette filters. Scott's Liquid Gold wood cleaner and preservative. Touch of Scent air freshener.

1081—Scovill, Inc., Pres. William F. Andrews, 500 Chase Pky., Waterbury, CT 06708, Phone 203-757-6061. **PRODUCTS:** Hamilton Beach housewares. Nutone housing products. Schrader auto products. Scovill apparel fasteners. Yale security products.

1083—Scripto, Inc., Chrm. Herbert W. Sams, P.O. Box 47800, Atlanta, GA 30362, Phone 404-447-5500. **PRODUCTS:**

Scripto Erasable ink pens, mechanical pencils, ball pens, china marking pencils, cigarette lighters, and fibertips.

1086—Seagram Company Ltd., Chrm. Edgar M. Brontman, 1430 Peel St., Montreal, Quebec, CANADA, H3A 1S9. **PRODUCTS:** Black Tower wine. Christian Brothers' wines. Paul Masson wines. Rhine light wine.

1087—Ohio-Sealy Mattress Manufacturing Co., Pres. Ernest M. Wuliger, 1300 E. 9th St., Cleveland, OH 44114, Phone 216-522-1310. **PRODUCTS:** Posturepedic mattress. Sealy mattresses.

1088—G.D. Searle & Company, Pres. Donald Rumsfeld, P. O. Box 1045, Skokie, IL 60076, Phone 312-982-7000. **PRODUCTS:** Nutri Sweet. Pearle Vision Eye Centers.

1089—Sears Roebuck & Company, Chrm. Edward R. Telling, Sears Tower, Chicago, IL 60684, Phone 312-875-2500. **PRODUCTS:** Allstate insurance. Dean Witter financial service. Kenmore appliances. Sears stores and products.

1090—Seiko Time Corporation, Pres. Robert Pliskin, 640 5th Ave., New York, NY 10019, Phone 212-977-2800. **PRODUCTS:** Seiko watches.

1092—Sentry Insurance, Chrm. John W. Joanis, 1800 N. Point Dr., Stevens Point, WI 54481, Phone 715-346-6000. **PRODUCTS:** Sentry insurance.

1093—Serta, Inc., Chrm. Donald S. Simon, 9801 W. Higgins Rd., Rosemont, IL 60018, Phone 312-692-6310. **PRODUCTS:** Serta mattresses.

1095—The Southland Corporation, Chrm. John P. Thompson, 2828 N. Haskell Ave., Dallas, TX 75204, Phone 214-828-7011. **PRODUCTS:** Chief auto parts. Citgo gasoline stations. Gristede supermarkets. Quik Mart convenience stores. 7-Eleven convenience stores.

1098—Sharp Electronics Corporation, Pres. K. Kubo, 10 Sharp Plaza, Paramus, NJ 07652, Phone 201-265-5600. **PRODUCTS:** Sharp computers, copiers, business machines, microwave ovens, televisions, video cassette recorders, and audio equipment.

1100—Shell Oil Company, Pres. J.F. Bookout, Box 2463, Houston, TX 77001, Phone 713-241-6161. **PRODUCTS:** Open Air room odorizer. Shell oil products. Shell pesticides.

1103—Sherwin-Williams Company, Chrm. John G. Breen, 101 Prospect Ave., N.W., Cleveland, OH 44115, Phone 216-566-2480. **PRODUCTS:** Dutch Boy paint. Sherwin-Williams paint and carpet.

1108—The Singer Company, Chrm. Joseph B. Flavin, P.O. Box 10151, Stamford, CT 06904, Phone 203-356-4200. **PRODUCTS:** Singer sewing machines.

1110—Emerson Electric Company, Chrm. C. F. Knight, 8000 W. Flourissant Ave., St. Louis, MO 63136, Phone 314-553-2000. **PRODUCTS:** Skil power tools.

1115—SmithKline Beckman Corporation, Chrm. Robert F. Dee, P.O. Box 7929, Philadelphia, PA 19101, Phone 215-751-4000. **PRODUCTS:** A.R.M. allergy medication. Benzedrex. Contac decongestant. Dietac diet pill. Ecotrin aspirin relief. Sine-Off decongestant. Teldrin antihistamine allergy pill.

1116—J.M. Smucker Company, Chrm. Paul H. Smucker, Strawberry Lane, Orrville, OH 44667, Phone 201-647-5800. **PRODUCTS:** Smucker's syrup, toppings, and jellies.

1120—Sony Corporation of America, Chrm. Norio Ohga, 9 W. 57th St., New York, NY 10019, Phone 212-371-5800. **PRODUCTS:** Sony electronic products.

1129—Sperry Corporation, Chrm. J. P. Lyet, 1290 Avenue of the Americas, New York, NY 10104, Phone 212-484-4444. **PRODUCTS:** Remington appliances. Remington shaver.

1132—Squibb Corporation, Chrm. Richard M. Furlaud, 40 W. 57th St., New York, NY 10019, Phone 212-621-7006. **PRODUCTS:** Bain de Soleil suntan lotion. Charles of the Ritz perfume. Enjoli perfume. Enjoli Midnite perfume. Jean Nate toiletries. Lanvin toiletries. Moisture Tanning Face Cream. Prescribe Nail Care. Rive Gauche perfume. Senchal perfume. Theragran-m. Yves St. Laurent cosmetics.

1136—Standard Oil Company of California, Chrm. G. M. Keller, 225 Bush, San Francisco, CA 94104, Phone 415-894-7700. **PRODUCTS:** Atlas batteries, tires, and accessories. Chevron petroleum products.

1141—The Stanley Works, Chrm. Donald W. Davis, 195 Lake St., New Britain, CT 06050, Phone 203-225-5111. **PRODUCTS:** Stanley tools, hardware, and garage door openers.

1143—State Farm Insurance, Pres. Edward B. Rust, One State Farm Plaza, Bloomington, IL 61701, Phone 309-766-2311. **PRODUCTS:** State Farm insurance.

1147—Stella D'Oro Bisquit Company, Chrm. Angela Kresevich, 184 W. 237th St., New York, NY 10463, Phone 212-549-3700. **PRODUCTS:** Stella D'Oro foods.

1148—Sterling Drug, Inc., Chrm. W. Clarke Wescoe, 90 Park Ave., New York, NY 10016, Phone 212-907-2000. **PRODUCTS:** Bayer aspirin. Beacon wax. Body All deodorant. Bowl Power automatic cleaner. Breacol cough syrup. Bronkaid asthma medication. Campho-Phenique medication. Chubs baby wipes. Cope pain medication. Cosprin pain medication. D-Con rodenticide. Diaparene Cushies towelettes. Double Power insecticide. Fletcher's Castoria laxative. Givenchy perfume. Haley's M-O. Lo-Sal antacid tablets. Love My Carpet. Lysol disinfectant. Midol pain medication. Mop & Glo floor cleaner. Neo-Synephrine decongestant. Ogilvie Home Permanent. Panadol pain reliever. Penetreat hair care. Perk floor wax. Phillips Milk of Magnesia. pHiso-Derm medicated cleanser. Pretty As A Picture air freshener. Stridex medicated pads. Tussy deodorant. Vanquish pain medication. Wet Ones moist towelettes.

1151—Stern's Garden Products, Inc., Pres. Horace Hagedorn, P.O. Box 888, Port Washington, NY 11050, Phone 516-883-6550. **PRODUCTS:** Miracle Gro fertilizer.

1155—Sarah Coventry, Inc., Chrm. Robert Catanzaro, Sarah Coventry Pky., Newark, NY 14593, Phone 315-331-6900. **PRODUCTS:** Sarah Coventry jewelry.

1159—Subaru of America, Inc., Pres. Harvey H. Lamm, 7040 Central Hwy., Pennsauken, NJ 08109, Phone 609-665-3344. **PRODUCTS:** Subaru automobiles.

1161—Sun Company, Inc., Chrm. Theodore A. Burtis, 100 Matsonford Rd., Radnor, PA 19087, Phone 215-293-6000. **PRODUCTS:** Sunoco gasoline.

1164—Sun-Maid Raisin Growers of California, Chrm. George Kaufman, 13525 S. Bethel Avenue, Kingsburg, CA 93631, Phone 209-896-8000. **PRODUCTS:** California raisins. Sun-Maid raisins.

1166—Sunkist Growers, Inc., Chrm. J.V. Newman, P.O. Box 7888, Van Nuys, CA 91409, Phone 213-986-4800. **PRODUCTS:** Sunkist oranges.

1173—TRW Inc., Chrm. R.F. Mettler, 23555 Euclid Ave., Cleveland, OH 44117, Phone 216-383-3246. **PRODUCTS:** TRW businesses.

1176—TAMPAX Inc., Pres. Edward H. Shutt, Jr., 10 Delaware Dr., Lake Success, NY 11042, Phone 516-437-8800. **PRODUCTS:** MAXITHINS sanitary pads. TAMPAX tampons.

1177—Tandy Corporation, Chrm. John V. Roach, 1900 One Tandy Ctr., Ft. Worth, TX 76102, Phone 817-390-3214. **PRODUCTS:** Memorex recording tape. Radio Shack stores, electronics, and computers.

1182—Teledyne Water Pik, Pres. David K. Mutchler, 1730 E. Prospect St., Fort Collins, CO 80525, Phone 303-484-

1352. **PRODUCTS:** One Step at a Time-Water Pik. Smart tip filters. Water Pik shower massage.

1184—Monroe Auto Equipment Company, Chrm. J.L. Ketelsen, International Dr., Monroe, MI 48161, Phone 313-243-8000. **PRODUCTS:** Monroe shock absorbers.

1185—Texaco, Inc., Chrm. John K. McKinley, 2000 Westchester Ave., White Plains, NY 10650, Phone 914-253-4000. **PRODUCTS:** Havoline oil. Texaco oil and gas products.

1186—Texas Instruments, Incorporated, Chrm. Mark Shepherd, Jr., P.O. Box 225474, Dallas, TX 75265, Phone 214-995-2011. **PRODUCTS:** Speak & Spell learning aid. Texas Instruments.

1187—Textron, Inc., Chrm. Robert P. Straetz, 40 Westminster St., Providence, RI 02818, Phone 401-421-2800. **PRODUCTS:** Allied paints. British Sterling aftershave. Home Lite chain saws. Speidel watch bands.

1191—Thompson Medical, Chrm. S. Daniel Abraham, 919 3rd Ave., New York, NY 10022, Phone 212-688-4420. **PRODUCTS:** Aspercreme analgesic creme rub. Control Diet pill. Dexatrim diet capsule. Pritikin low-salt foods. Prolamine Slimfast diet aid. Sportscreme ointment. Ultra Lean diet aid.

1193—Time Incorporated, Chrm. Ralph P. Davidson, Time & Life Bldg., Rockefeller Center, New York, NY 10020, Phone 212-586-1212. **PRODUCTS:** Book-of-the-Month Club. Cinemax pay cable service. Discover magazine. Fortune magazine. Great American Reserve Insurance Co. Home

Box Office. People Magazine. QPB books. Sports Illustrated magazine. Time Life books. Time magazine.

1195—Timex Corporation, Chrm. Fred Olsen, 1579 Straits Turnpike, Middlebury, CT 06762, Phone 203-573-5000. **PRODUCTS:** Healthcheck instruments. Timex watches and clocks.

1196—Tomy Corporation, Pres. David T. Iida, P.O. Box 6252, Carson, CA 90749, Phone 213-549-2721. **PRODUCTS:** Big Loader Construction Set. Mr. Mouth game. Pencil Pets.

1197—Tonka Corporation, Pres. Stephen G. Shank, 4144 Shoreline Blvd., Spring Park, MN 55384, Phone 612-475-9500. **PRODUCTS:** Tonka toys.

1198—Tootsie Roll Industries, Inc., Chrm. Melvin J. Gordon, 7401 S. Cicero Ave., Chicago, IL 60629, Phone 312-581-6100. **PRODUCTS:** Bonomo Turkish Taffee. Mason Dots & Crows. Tootsie Pops. Tootsie Roll candy.

1205—Toyota Motor Sales, Pres. I. Makino, 19001 S. Western Ave., Torrance, CA 90509, Phone 213-618-4000. **PRODUCTS:** Toyota motor vehicles.

1207—Trans World Corporation, Chrm. L. Edwin Smart, 605 3rd Ave., New York, NY 10158, Phone 212-557-5500. **PRODUCTS:** Century 21 real estate. Trans World Airlines.

1208—Transamerica Corporation, Pres. James R. Harvey, 600 Montgomery St., San Francisco, CA 94111, Phone 415-983-4000. **PRODUCTS:** Transamerica Insurance.

1217—Turtle Wax, Inc., Pres. Denis J. Healy, 5655 W.

77th Street, Chicago, IL 60638, Phone 312-284-8300. **PRODUCTS:** Minute Wax. Turtle Wax.

1219—Tyson Foods, Incorporated, Chrm. Don Tyson, 2210 W. Oaklawn Dr., Springdale, AR 72764, Phone 501-756-4000. **PRODUCTS:** Tyson Breast of Chicken.

1220—United Air Lines, Pres. Richard J. Ferris, Box 66100, Chicago, IL 60666, Phone 312-952-4000. **PRODUCTS:** United Air Express. United Airlines.

1224—Lever Brothers, Chrm. Michael R. Angus, 390 Park Ave., New York, NY 10022, Phone 212-688-6000. **PRODUCTS:** Aim toothpaste. All detergent. Breeze detergent. Caress soap. Close-Up toothpaste. Denim after shave. Dimension shampoo. Dove detergent. Dove soap. Drive detergent. DX toothbrush. Final Touch fabric conditioner. Imperial margarine. Impulse body spray. Kjirst malt beverage. Lifebuoy soap. Lifeline Professional toothbrushes. Lux dishwashing detergents. Lux soap. Mrs. Butterworth's syrup. Pepsodent toothbrushes. Pepsodent toothpaste. Pepsodent tooth powder. Phase III soap. Praise soap. Promise spreads. Rinso detergent. Shield soap. Signal mouthwash. Snuggle liquid fabric softener. Sunlight dishwashing liquid. Swan dishwashing detergent. Trim diet soup mixes. Twice as Nice shampoo. Wisk detergent.

1225—Union Carbide Corporation, Chrm. Warren M. Anderson, Old Ridgebury Rd., Danbury, CT 06817, Phone 203-794-2000. **PRODUCTS:** Energizer batteries. Eveready batteries. Glad plastic bags. Glad Wrap. Prestone antifreeze. Simonize car care products. Union Carbide.

1227—Union Oil Company of California, Chrm. Fred L. Hartley, P.O. Box 7600, Los Angeles, CA 90051, Phone 213-977-7600. **PRODUCTS:** Union Oil Company.

1228—Uniroyal, Inc., Chrm. Joseph P. Flannery, World Headquarters, Middlebury, CT 06749, Phone 203-573-2000. **PRODUCTS:** Uniroyal tires.

1230—United Brands Company, Chrm. Seymour Milstein, 1271 Avenue of the Americas, New York, NY 10020, Phone 212-397-4000. **PRODUCTS:** A & W root beer and fast food. Chiquita bananas.

1232—Write Your Congressman and Senator. Congressman in care of U.S. House of Representatives, Washington, DC 20515. Senator in care of U.S. Senate, Washington, DC 20510. **PRODUCTS:** United States Air Force. United States Armed Forces. United States Army. United States Marines. United States Navy. United States Armed Services.

1244—U. S. Shoe Corporation, Chrm. Philip G. Barach, One Eastwood Dr., Cincinnati, OH 45227, Phone 513-527-7000. **PRODUCTS:** Bill Blass shoes. Capezio shoes. Cobbies shoes. Evan-Picone shoes. Freeman shoes. Imperial shoes. Liz Claiborne shoes. Pappagallo shoes. Texas Steer boots.

1247—U. S. Suzuki Motor Corporation, Pres. Y. Tekeuchi, 3251 E. Imperial Hwy., Brea, CA 92621, Phone 714-996-7040. **PRODUCTS:** Suzuki motor vehicles.

1248—U.S. Tobacco Company, Chrm. Louis F. Bantle, 100 W. Putnam Ave., Greenwich, CT 06830, Phone 203-661-1100. **PRODUCTS:** Cedar King pencils. Charley pens. Dills pipe cleaners. Dr. Granow pipes. Honor Roll pencils. Mustang pens. Nawico wines. Pommerelle wines. Ste. Michelle wines. **TOBACCO PRODUCTS:** Amphora Blend Eleven. Bandits smokeless tobacco. Bond Street. Borkum Riff. Briggs. Bruton. CC. Copenhagen smokeless tobacco. Don Tomas. Field & Stream. Happy Days smokeless tobacco. House of Windsor. Key. Mapleton. Mark IV. Red Seal. Revelation. Right Cut. Rooster. Skoal Bandits smokeless tobacco. Skoal smokeless tobacco. Standard. Union Leader. WB Cut. Wolf Brothers.

1251—The Upjohn Company, Chrm. R. T. Parfet, Jr., 7000 Portage Rd., Kalamazoo, MI 49001, Phone 616-323-4000. **PRODUCTS:** Cortaid. Unicap vitamins.

1253—V.F. Corporation, Chrm. Robert H. Andrews, 1047 N. Park Rd., Reading, PA 19610, Phone 215-378-1151. **PRODUCTS:** Lee jeans.

1260—Volkswagen of America, Pres. Noel Phillips, 27621 Parkview Blvd., Warren, MI 48092, Phone 313-362-6000. **PRODUCTS:** Audi automobiles. Porsche automobiles. Volkswagen automobiles.

1262—Volvo of America Corporation, Pres. Bjorn Ahlstrom, Rockleigh Industrial Park, Rockleigh, NJ 07647, Phone 201-768-7300. **PRODUCTS:** Volvo automobiles.

1264—Wagner Spray Tech Corporation, Pres. Udo E. Schulz, 1770 Fernbrook Lane, Minneapolis, MN 55441, Phone 612-559-1770. **PRODUCTS:** Wagner Power Sprayer.

1266—Walgreen Company, Chrm. C. R. Walgreen III, 200 Wilmot Rd., Deerfield, IL 60015, Phone 312-948-5000. **PRODUCTS:** Walgreen Drug Stores.

1270—Wang Laboratories, Inc., Chrm. An Wang, One Industrial Ave., Lowell, MA 01851, Phone 617-459-5000. **PRODUCTS:** Wang Labs computers, word processing systems, and office automation equipment.

1271—The Terson Company, Inc., Chrm. Joe A. Masterson, 310 S. Michigan Ave., Chicago, IL 60604, Phone 312-461-9111. **PRODUCTS:** Bit-O-Honey candy. Johnston's pies. Roman Meal bread.

1273—Warner Communications, Chrm. Steven J. Ross, 75 Rockefeller Plaza. New York, NY 10019, Phone 212-484-8000. **PRODUCTS:** Atari games. Chaps cologne. Franklin Mint collector items. Gloria Vanderbilt jeans. Gloria Vanderbilt perfume. Warner Communications products.

1274—Warner-Lambert Company, Chrm. Ward S. Hagan, 201 Tabor Rd., Morris Plains, NJ 07950, Phone 201-540-2000. **PRODUCTS:** Adams gum. Allercreme. Beemans gum. Benylin cough syrup. Bountiful snack foods. Bromo Seltzer antacid. Bubblicious gum. Certs breath mints. Chewels gum. Chiclets gum. Clorets breath fresheners. Corn Husker's body lotion. Dentyne chewing gum. Dynamints candy. Efferdent denture cleaner. Effergrip denture adhesive. Freshen-up gum. Halls cough drops. Listerine mouthwash. Listermint mouthwash. Lubriderm lotion. Myadec vitamins. Personal Touch lady razor. Rolaids antacid. Schick Super II razor. Sinutabs medication. Spring chewing gum. Trident chewing gum. Ultrex blades.

1280—National Grape Co-op Association, Inc., Pres. J. Roy Orton, 2 S. Portage St., Westfield, NY 14787, Phone 716-326-3131. **PRODUCTS:** Welch's grape products.

1282—Wella Corporation, Pres. George H. Megerle, 524 Grand Ave., Englewood, NJ 07631, Phone 201-569-1020. **PRODUCTS:** Wella hair products.

1286—Wendy's International, Chrm. Robert L. Barney, Box 256, Dublin, OH 43017, Phone 614-764-3100. **PRODUCTS:** Sisters Chicken & Biscuits fast food. Wendy's hamburgers.

1287—Western Airlines, Chrm. Larry Lee, 6060 Avion Dr., Los Angeles, CA 90045, Phone 213-646-2345. **PRODUCTS:** Western Airlines.

1288—Best Western International, Inc., CEO Ron Evans, P.O. Box 10203, Phoenix, AZ 85064, Phone 602-957-4200. **PRODUCTS:** Best Western motels. Milford Plaza Hotel.

1291—Westinghouse Electric Corporation, Chrm. Robert E. Kirby, Westinghouse Building Gateway Center, Pittsburgh, PA 15222, Phone 412-255-3800. **PRODUCTS:** Westinghouse products.

1294—Whirlpool Corporation, Chrm. Jack D. Sparks, Administrative Center, Benton Harbor, MI 44111, Phone 616-926-5000. **PRODUCTS:** Whirlpool appliances.

1297—White Consolidated Industries, Inc., Chrm. Roy H. Holdt, 11770 Berea Rd., Cleveland, OH 44111, Phone 216-252-3700 **PRODUCTS:** Frigidaire appliances.

1302—Wm. Wrigley Jr. Company, Pres. William Wrigley, 410 N. Michigan Ave., Chicago, IL 60611, Phone 312-644-2121. **PRODUCTS:** Big Red gum. Doublemint chewing gum. Freedent gum. Hubba Bubba gum. Juicyfruit chewing gum. Orbit gum. Wrigley's chewing gum.

1304—Mott's Super Markets, Inc., Chrm. Joseph P. Mott, 59-63 Leggett St., East Hartford, CT 06108, Phone 203-289-3301. **PRODUCTS:** Giacobazzi wines.

1308—Witco Chemical Corporation, Chrm. William Wishnick, 520 Madison Ave., New York, NY 10022, Phone 212-605-3800. **PRODUCTS:** Kendall Oil products.

1309—Wolverine World Wide, Inc., Chrm. Thomas D. Gleason, 9341 Courtland Dr., Rockford, MI 49351, Phone 616-866-1561. **PRODUCTS:** Hush Puppies shoes.

1313—Kinney Shoe Corporation, Pres. R.L. Anderson, 233 Broadway, New York, NY 10279, Phone 212-553-2000. **PRODUCTS:** Kinney Shoes.

1319—Xerox Corporation, Chrm. David T. Kearns, P.O. Box 1600, Stamford, CT 06904, Phone 203-329-8700. **PRODUCTS:** Xerox office machines and supplies.

1321—Yamaha Motor Corporation, U.S.A., Pres. T. Kimura, 6555 Katella Ave., Cypress, CA 90630, Phone 714-522-9011. **PRODUCTS:** Yamaha motorcycles.

1324—W. F. Young, Inc., Pres. Wilbur F. Young, 111 Lyman St., Springfield, MA 01101, Phone 413-737-0201. **PRODUCTS:** Absorbine Jr. liniment.

1325—Zale Corporation, Chrm. Donald Zale, 3000 Diamond Park Dr., Dallas, TX 75247, Phone 214-634-4011. **PRODUCTS:** Zales stores.

1327—Zenith Radio Corporation, Chrm. Walter C. Fisher, 1000 N. Milwaukee Ave., Glenview, IL 60025, Phone 312-391-7000. **PRODUCTS:** Zenith microcomputers, television sets, and electronics.

1330—Zippo Manufacturing Company, Chrm. Robert D. Galey, 33 Barbour St., Bradford, PA 16701, Phone 814-362-4541. **PRODUCTS:** Zippo lighters.

1333—Hewlett-Packard Company, Pres. John A. Young, 3000 Hanover St., Palo Alto, CA 94304, Phone 415-857-1501. **PRODUCTS:** Hewlett-Packard electronics and computers.

1335—Pentax Corporation, Chrm. K. Chiwata, 35 Inverness Dr. E., Englewood, CO 80112, Phone 303-773-1101. **PRODUCTS:** Pentax binoculars, Pentax cameras. Pentax video.

1339—Hitachi America, Ltd., Pres. Katsuaki Suzuki, 437 Madison Ave., New York, NY 10022, Phone 212-758-5420. **PRODUCTS:** Hitachi electronics.

1340—American Greeting Corporation, Chrm. Irving I. Stone, 10500 American Rd., Cleveland, OH 44144, Phone 216-252-7300. **PRODUCTS:** American Greeting cards.

1341—Tree Top, Inc., Pres. Dennis J. Colleran, 2nd & Railroad Ave., Selah, WA 98942, Phone 509-697-7251. **PRODUCTS:** Sparkling Cider. Sparkling Royale juices. Tree Top apple juice.

1343—Robbins & Myers, Inc., Chrm. Maynard H. March IV, 1400 Winter Bank Tower, Dayton, OH 45402, Phone 573-222-2610. **PRODUCTS:** Hunter fans.

1345—Triumph-Adler, Chrm. Robert Hagy, P.O. 92300, Los Angeles, CA 90009, Phone 213-642-4601. **PRODUCTS:** Adler business machines. Royal business machines.

1346—El Greco Leather Products, Chrm. Charles Cole, 2 Harbor Park Dr., Port Washington, NY 11050, Phone 212-246-5830. **PRODUCTS:** Candies shoes.

1347—Weber-Stephen Products, Chrm. George Stephens, 100 N. Hickory, Arlington, IL 60004, Phone 312-259-5010. **PRODUCTS:** One Touch. Weber grills.

1350—Jovan Incorporated, Chrm. Bernard A. Mitchell, 875 N. Michigan Ave., Chicago, IL 60611, Phone 312-951-7000. **PRODUCTS:** Andron cologne. Gambler fragrance. Glacier men's after-shave. Jovan toiletries. Lady fragrance. Laughter perfume. Liquid Cream Soap. Vitabath bath products. Yardley soaps.

1351—Thomas J. Lipton, Inc., Pres. H.M. Tibbetts, 800 Sylvan Ave., Englewood Cliffs, NJ 07632, Phone 614-888-9280. **PRODUCTS:** Bite-Size Tabby cat food. Classic dressing. Knox gelatine. Lipton Egg Noodle. Lipton tea and soups. Total Dinner cat food. Wish-Bone salad dressing.

1352—Chanel, Inc., President Kitty D'Alessio, 9 W. 57th St., New York, NY 10019, Phone 212-688-5055. **PRODUCTS:** Chanel perfume.

1353—Jartran Truck Rentals, President Kevin Murphy, 3001 Ponce de Leon Blvd., Coral Gables, FL 33134, Phone 305-448-8788. **PRODUCTS:** Jartran truck rentals.

1354—Activision, Inc., Pres. Jim Levy, Drawer No. 7286, Mountain View, CA 94042, Phone 408-942-1370. **PRODUCTS:** Activision video cartridges. Megomania video game.

1355—American Isuzu Motors, Ltd., Pres. Yukio Itagaki, 2300 Pellissier Place, Whittier, CA 90601, Phone 213-949-0611. **PRODUCTS:** Isuzu automobiles.

1356—Tiger International, Inc., Chrm. Wayne M. Hoffman, 1888 Century Pk. E, Los Angeles, CA 90067, Phone 213-552-6300. **PRODUCTS:** Flying Tiger Air Line.

1357—Kero-Sun, Incorporated, Pres. Bill Litwin, Kent, CT 06757, Phone 203-927-4611. **PRODUCTS:** Kero-Sun heaters.

1358—Imagic Corporation, Pres. William Grubb, 981 University Ave., Los Gates, CA 95030, Phone 408-399-2200. **PRODUCTS:** Demon Attack video game. Dragonfire video game. Ice Trek video game. Imagic video games. Microsurgeon video game. No Escape video game. Riddle of the Sphinx video game. Shootin' Gallery video game. Sword and Serpents video game. Trick Shot video game. Truckin' video game. Star Voyager video game.

1359—Sentry Hardware Company, Managing Director Dick Brant, 33 Public Sq., Cleveland, OH 44113, Phone 216-621-2045. **PRODUCTS:** Sentry Hardware stores.

1360—First Jersey Securities, Chrm. Robert Brennan, 50th Broadway, 14th Floor, New York, NY 10004, Phone 212-269-5500. **PRODUCTS:** First Jersey financial securities.

1362—Turco Kerosene Company, President Robert Feigenbaum,

501 S. Line St., DuQuoin, IL 62832, Phone 618-542-4781. **PRODUCTS:** Turco kerosene heaters.

1363—Smith Barney, Harris Upham & Co., Inc., President John A. Orb, 1345 Avenue of the Americas, New York, NY 10105, Phone 212-399-6000. **PRODUCTS:** Smith-Barney financial services.

1364—Van Munching & Company, Chrm. Leo Van Munching, Jr., 51 W. 51st St., New York, NY 10019, Phone 212-265-2685. **PRODUCTS:** Heinekein beer.

1365—American Gas Association, Executive Director John Clark, 1515 Wilson Blvd., Arlington, VA 22209, Phone 703-841-8400. **PRODUCTS:** American Gas Association.

1366—Commodore International Limited, Chrm. Irving Gould, 950 Rittenhouse Road, Norristown, PA 19403, Phone 215-666-7950. **PRODUCTS:** Commodore computers. Vic 20 Commodore computers.

1368—Apple Computer, Incorporated, Chrm. A.C. Markkula, Jr., 10260 Bandley Dr., Cupertino, CA 95014, Phone 408-996-1010. **PRODUCTS:** Apple computers.

1370—Krazy Glue, Incorporated, Chrm. Henry Jadow, 53 W. 23rd St., New York, NY 10010, Phone 212-807-3844. **PRODUCTS:** Krazy Glue.

1372—TSR Hobbies, Incorporated, Chrm. Brian Blume, Post Office Box 756, Lake Geneva, WI 53147, Phone 414-248-3625. **PRODUCTS:** Dungeons and Dragons video games. Star Frontiers video games. TSR hobbies and video games.

1374—Nikon Incorporated, Pres. Herbert Sax, 623 Stewart Ave., Garden City, NJ 11530, Phone 516-222-0200. **PRODUCTS:** Nikon cameras.

1375—Schaper Manufacturing Company, Pres. W. L. Garrity, 9909 S. Shore Dr., Minneapolis, MN 55441, Phone 612-540-0511. **PRODUCTS:** Playmobil toys. Schaper toys.

1376—Thorn EMI Home Video, Chrm. Gary Dartnell, 1370 Avenue of the Americas, New York, NY 10019, Phone 212-977-8990. **PRODUCTS:** Thorn EMI computer games and video cassettes.

1377—Twentieth Century Fox Films Corporation, Chrm. Alan J. Hirschfield, P.O. Box 900, Beverly Hills, CA 90213, Phone 213-277-2211. **PRODUCTS:** 20th Century Fox films.

1378—MCA Incorporated, Chrm. L.R. Wasserman, 100 University Plaza, Universal City, CA 91601, Phone 213-985-4321. **PRODUCTS:** Universal Motion Pictures

1379—Digital Equipment Corporation, President Kenneth H. Olsen, 146 Main Street, Maynard, MA 01754, Phone 617-897-5111. **PRODUCTS:** Digital electronic computing equipment.

1380—MGM/UA Entertainment Company, Chrm. F.E. Rosenfelt, 10202 W. Washington Blvd., Culver City, CA 90230, Phone 213-558-5000. **PRODUCTS:** MGM/UA movie and television productions.

1381—TeleFlora, Incorporated, Pres. Stewart Resnick, 2400 Compton Blvd., Redondo Beach, CA 90278, Phone 213-973-2501. **PRODUCTS:** Tele-Flora flower delivery.

1382—Marriott Corporation, Chrm. J. Willard Marriott, Jr., Marriott Dr., Washington, DC 20058, Phone 301-897-9000. **PRODUCTS:** Marriott hotels.

1383—International Games, Inc., Chrm. Bob Tezak, One Uno Circle, Joliet, IL 60435, Phone 815-741-4000. **PRODUCTS:** Uno cards.

1384—Ricoh of America, Chrm. Hisashi Kubo, 20 Gloria Lane, Fairfield, NJ 07006, Phone 201-575-9550. **PRODUCTS:** Ricoh Copier Machine 4060.

1385—NCL Cruise Lines, Chrm. Ronald Zeller, #1 Biscayne Tower, Miami, FL 33131, Phone 305-358-6670. **PRODUCTS:** NCL Cruise Lines.

1386—Levolor Lorentzen, Inc., Chrm. Clinton Gibbs, 1280 Wallstreet W., Lindhurst, NJ 07071, Phone 201-460-8400. **PRODUCTS:** Levolor blinds.

1388—Independent Insurance Agents, Executive V.P. Jeffery Yates, 100 Church St., New York, NY 10007, Phone 212-285-4250. **PRODUCTS:** Independent Insurance Agents.

1389—Fuji Photo Film Company, Ltd., Pres. Bernie Yasunaga, 350 Fifth Ave., New York, NY 10118, Phone 212-736-3335. **PRODUCTS:** Fuji film. Fuji magnetic tapes.

1391—Allied Corporation, Chrm. Edward L. Hennessy, Jr., P.O. Box 4000R, Morristown, NJ 07960, Phone 201-455-2000. **PRODUCTS:** Anso IV carpet. Autolite spark plugs. Bendix products. FRAM auto parts.

1392—Boehringer Ingelheim Ltd., Pres. Harvey Sadow, 90 E. Ridge, Ridgefield, CT 06877, Phone 203-438-0311. **PRODUCTS:** Alupent Mist Inhaler. Dulcolax laxative.

1393—Bridgestone Tire Co. of America, Pres. Kunio Satake, 2000 W. 190th, Torrance, CA 90509, Phone 213-320-6030. **PRODUCTS:** Bridgestone tires.

1394—Days Inns of America, Inc., Chrm. Cecil B. Day, 2751 Buford Hwy., Atlanta, GA 30324, Phone 404-325-4000. **PRODUCTS:** Days Inns.

1395—Pro-Line Corporation, Chrm. Comer J. Cotrell, 2121 Panoramic Circle, Dallas, TX 75212, Phone 214-631-4247. **PRODUCTS:** Curly Kit.

1396—Anglers Co. Limited, Pres. Gerson Strassberg, 45-25 162nd St., Flushing, NY 11357, Phone 212-961-7744. **PRODUCTS:** Protectall clear vinyl sheet protector.

1397—Mirror Bright Polish Company, Chrm. Malcolm Meguian, 17275 Daimer, Irvine, CA 92713, Phone 714-557-9200. **PRODUCTS:** Mequiar's Fast Finish car polish.

1398—Jordache. Chrm. Joseph Nakash, 498 7th Ave., New York, NY 10018, Phone 212-279-7343. **PRODUCTS:** Jordache clothing.

1503—TDK Electronics Corporation, Pres. Fukujiro Sono, 12 Harbor Park Dr., Port Washington, NY 11050, Phone 516-746-0880. **PRODUCTS:** TDK recording tape.

1510—Converse, Inc., Chrm. Richard Loynd, 55 Fordham Road, Wilmington, MA 01887, Phone 617-657-5500. **PRODUCTS:** Converse athletic shoes.

1529—Pioneer Electronics, Chrm. Jack Doyle, P.O. Box 54, Long Beach, CA 90801, Phone 213-639-5050. **PRODUCTS:** Pioneer stereo equipment.